# THE
# SCOTTISH
# COLLECTION
# OF VERSE
## TO 1800

# THE
# SCOTTISH
# COLLECTION
# OF VERSE
## TO 1800

*Compiled by*
*Eileen Dunlop and Antony Kamm*

*RICHARD DREW PUBLISHING*
*Glasgow*

First published 1985 by
Richard Drew Publishing Ltd
6 Clairmont Gardens, Glasgow G3 7LW

ISBN 0 86267 143 4 (cased)
0 86267 142 6 (limp)

British Library Cataloguing in Publication Data

The Scottish collection of verse.
 Vol. 1
 1. English poetry — Scottish authors
 I. Dunlop, Eileen    II. Kamm, Antony
 821'.008'09411    PR8651

 ISBN 0 86267 143 4
 ISBN 0 86267 142 6 Pbk

Designed by James W Murray

Set in Scantext Ehrhardt by
John Swain & Son Limited, Glasgow
Printed by Blantyre Printing & Binding Co. Ltd.

# *Contents*

Introduction, 11

*People and Places*, 13

The Braes o' Ballochmyle · Robert Burns, 15
Amends to the Tailors and Shoemakers · William Dunbar, 15
Epigram · Allan Ramsay, 17
Satire on the Town Ladies · Sir Richard Maitland, 17
To a Lady · Robert Burns, 21
Sir William Wallace, 21
Holy Willie's Prayer · Robert Burns, 24
*From* A Satire of the Three Estates · Sir David Lyndsay, 27
*From* Ben Dorain · Duncan Ban MacIntyre, 30
The Daft Days · Robert Fergusson, 33
In Orkney · William Fowler, 35
Banishment · Mary Macleod, 36
Logan Braes · John Mayne, 37
The Braes o' Menstrie, 38
It is Time for me to Go up into the House of Paradise, 38

*Kings and Queens*, 39

'When Alysandyr our King was Dede', 41
*From* Sir William Wallace · Blind Harry, 42
Scots Wha Hae · Robert Burns, 43
*From* The Kingis Quair · James I, 44
Remonstrance to the King · William Dunbar, 46
An Exhortation to His Grace the King · Sir David Lyndsay, 49
*From* A New Year Gift to the Queen Mary · Alexander Scott, 52
The Queen's Marie, 53
Sonnet · James VI, 56

To Queen Anne · Sir Robert Ayton, 57
*From* An Exhortation to Prince Henry · Sir William Alexander, 58
On the Prince's Death · Sir Robert Ayton, 59
To Prince Charles · Sir William Alexander, 60
Lines on the Execution of King Charles I · Marquis of Montrose, 60

## *Nature, Birds, Animals,* 61

*From* The Cherrie and the Slae · Alexander Montgomerie, 63
*From* Of a Summer's Day · Alexander Hume, 65
*From* The Seasons · James Thomson, 68
On Seeing a Butterfly in the Street · Robert Fergusson, 69
To a Mouse · Robert Burns, 72
The Tale of the Country Mouse and the
   Town Mouse · Robert Henryson, 74
The Chamaeleon · Allan Ramsay, 81
The Clipping Blessing, 82
A Song of Foxes · Duncan Ban MacIntyre, 83
Translation of the
   Death of a Sparrow · William Drummond, 85
Ode to the Gowdspink · Robert Fergusson, 87
To a Mountain Daisy · Robert Burns, 90

## *The Sea,* 93

Sir Patrick Spens, 95
*From* The Aeneid · Gavin Douglas, 99
*From* The Shipwreck · William Falconer, 100
*From* A Saturday's Expedition · Robert Fergusson, 102
Rule Britannia · David Mallet, 104
The Lowlands of Holland, 106
*From* The Birlinn of Clanranald · Alexander Macdonald, 107
Sea Prayer, 108

## *Food and Drink,* 111

To a Haggis · Robert Burns, 113
*From* Rauf Coilyear, 114
Caller Herrin' · Lady Nairne, 116
Caller Oysters · Robert Fergusson, 117
Elegy on Lucky Wood · Allan Ramsay, 120
Lord Donald, 122
'Wha Hes Gud Malt', 124
Song to the Brandy · Duncan Ban MacIntyre, 125

## *Sport and Entertainment,* 127

'The Bewteis of the Fute-Ball', 129
*From* A Winter Season · James Fisher, 129
*From* Christ's Kirk on the Grene, 130
Song on Missing at Hunting · Duncan Ban MacIntyre, 132
Leith Races · Allan Ramsay, 134
Elegy on the Death of Scots Music · Robert Fergusson, 135
Prologue Spoken by Mr Anthony Alston · Allan Ramsay, 138
The Canongate Playhouse in Ruins · Robert Fergusson, 139

## *War,* 143

*From* The Bruce · John Barbour, 145
Battle of Otterbourne, 146
The Flowers of the Forest · Jean Elliot, 151
The Day of Inverlochy · Iain Lom, 152
The Hundred Pipers · Lady Nairne, 155
Johnnie Cope · Adam Skirving, 156
My Love's in Germany · Colonel Thomas Traill, 158
The Silver Tassie · Robert Burns, 159
'O Where, Tell me Where' · Ann Grant of Laggan, 160
Bonnie George Campbell, 161
On Thanksgiving for a National Victory · Robert Burns, 161

*Love,* 163

A Red, Red Rose · Robert Burns, 165
To his Mistress · Alexander Montgomerie, 166
Doun the Burn, Davie · Robert Crawford, 166
*From* The Gentle Shepherd · Allan Ramsay, 167
The Blue-Eyed Lassie · Robert Burns, 168
Sonnet · William Fowler, 169
To his Mistress · John Stewart of Baldynneis, 170
O, Wert Thou in the Cauld Blast · Robert Burns, 171
'The Tender Snow, of Granis Soft and
    Quhyt' · Alexander Montgomerie, 172
Annie Laurie · Douglas of Fingland, 172
On Love · Sir Robert Ayton, 173
'Werena my Heart Licht I wad Dee' · Lady Grisell Baillie, 174
Madrigal · William Drummond, 175
*From* The Testament of Cresseid · Robert Henryson, 176
Come under my Plaidie · Hector MacNeill, 178
Ye Banks and Braes · Robert Burns, 179
O Waly, Waly, 180
Auld Robin Gray · Lady Anne Barnard, 181
Secret Love · Isabel Stewart, 183
John Anderson my Jo · Robert Burns, 184
To Love, Unloved · Alexander Scott, 185
Genty Tibby and Sonsy Nelly · Allan Ramsay, 186
'When Flora had Ourfret the Firth', 187
On Platonic Love · Sir Robert Ayton, 188
Blythe was She · Robert Burns, 190


*Religion,* 191

A Song of the Birth of Christ, 193
Of Christ's Nativity · William Dunbar, 195
In Dulci Jubilo, 197

Of Christ's Resurrection · William Dunbar, 197
Psalm 23, 199
Psalm 124, 200
Psalm 130 · Robert Ker, 201
Think on God, 202
Prayer · Muireadhach Albannach, 202
'My Lufe Murnis for Me', 203
A Prayer, under the Pressure of
    Violent Anguish · Robert Burns, 204
A Prayer against the Plague · Robert Henryson, 205
Rune of Hospitality, 208

## *Death*, 209

The Twa Corbies, 211
'Lament for the Makaris' · William Dunbar, 212
Written on the Eve of his Execution · Marquis of Montrose, 215
O Happie Death · Alexander Hume, 216
The Land o' the Leal · Lady Nairne, 216
Tam the Chapman · Robert Burns, 217
Bessie Bell and Mary Gray, 218
Epitaph, Intended for Himself · James Beattie, 218
My Last Will · Robert Fergusson, 219
On James Smith · Robert Burns, 222
On the Death of Mr Thomas Lancashire,
    Comedian · Robert Fergusson, 222
The Bonny Earl o' Moray, 223
The Lament of the Border Widow, 224
Rare Willy Drowned in Yarrow, 225
A Lyke-Wake Dirge, 225

## *The Supernatural*, 227

Sweet William's Ghost, 229
Tam o' Shanter · Robert Burns, 232

The Earl of Mar's Daughter, 238
Up in the Air · Allan Ramsay, 243
The Grey Selchie, 244
Thomas the Rhymer, 245
Omens, 248
The Wife of Usher's Well, 248
The Hazlewood Witch · Richard Gall, 250
Fine Flowers in the Valley · Robert Burns, 251

Index of first lines and ballad titles, 252
Index of poets, 256

# *Introduction*

*When the 18th century ended, Robert Burns was dead and Sir Walter Scott, the next Scottish literary "giant" in time, had not yet published any verse of his own. Nor had James Hogg. For those reasons, 1800 is a suitable terminus ad quem. Other writers whose lives spanned the two centuries have been included where the poems were written, or likely to have been written, before 1800.*

*Even so, there are some five centuries of verse writing to be covered, and poets of the rank of Barbour, Dunbar, Henryson, Alexander Montgomerie, Alexander Scott, Fergusson, Allan Ramsay and Burns himself, to be fairly represented, as well as Gaelic verse, and the anonymous "makaris" and ballad composers. The themes by which the pieces are arranged are those which seem over the centuries to have influenced much of Scottish life, history and attitudes, as well as literature. The poems, or complete extracts from longer poems, have been chosen simply because they appeal to us and seem appropriately to illuminate a particular theme. An anthology is an eminently personal thing, for compilers and readers alike, and so we can only hope that anyway much of what we have enjoyed will give pleasure also to others. And that what can be of each author or of Scottish verse of the period only a sip, will still in most cases give a taste which is not uncharacteristic.*

*The question of language has exercised us as much as it has other anthologists. Any solution can only be partial, or a compromise. However, the fact that much of the greatest Scottish poetry of the 17th and 18th centuries is in Scots is actually an advantage when it comes to offering also equally evocative Middle Scots poems. Once one starts fiddling with accepted texts, it is difficult to know when to stop, or to stop. So we have left the texts as we have found them, though in deference to the typesetter we have rendered the medieval "ʒ" as "y"; and we have modernised a few titles of poems where we felt this would be especially helpful. However, we have added to the poems in Middle Scots, which means roughly anything written before about 1600, marginal glosses where we thought these would be particularly*

11

appropriate, and we hope that they will enable the general reader to gain as much pleasure from these poems as from those written in English or Scots. Reading them aloud, and slowly, will often resolve some of the apparent problems caused by the erratic spelling of the times. Otherwise, bear in mind that "wh" is often printed as "quh"; that "v" and "u" are interchangeable; that "scho" is "she"; and "erd" means "earth".

Gaelic poetry is represented in 19th-century translations into English verse, in the choice of which we employed the same criteria as for the selection of all the other poems.

*Eileen Dunlop and Antony Kamm*
*Dollar, July 1985*

# *People and Places*

*The Scots have celebrated the raw grandeur and infinite variety of their lands and countryside almost since they began to write poetry. Robert Burns deliberately set out to reflect Scottish poetic tradition, and saw it as his responsibility to write of his native Ayrshire countryside, which he felt had received scant poetic notice. Not far from the Braes of Ballochmyle are Logan Braes, the subject of John Mayne's poem, from which incidentally Burns lifted two lines for a poem on the same subject. The equally romantic but more robust strain of the Gaelic poet, Duncan Ban MacIntyre, in his Ben Dorain, has its contrast in the Edinburgh poems of Robert Fergusson, of which The Daft Days describes the traditional New Year jollities.*

*On what occasion William Fowler, one-time spy in France for the Protestant cause and latterly secretary to Queen Mary, wife of James VI, visited Orkney is not known, but his poem graphically reflects the isolation and elemental nature of an island existence. A different kind of island isolation is described by Mary Macleod, in her poem addressed to the chief who had banished her from her home on Skye. Happily, he did relent, and brought her home. There is some doubt as to exactly when and for how long she lived, but reputable sources suggest she really did die at the age of 105 and that she was, to the last, an energetic and bibulous body.*

*Another traditional feature of Scottish verse is its humour — wicked, satirical, gay or grim. All these facets are represented here among the poems about people. William Dunbar, ostensibly writing to redress a wrong, cannot resist a last-verse dig at the subjects of his poem. Sir Richard Maitland was about sixty and going blind when he started writing poetry, which may have affected his judgment, but certainly not his powers of observation or his sense of humour. The short verses by Burns and Allan Ramsay prove, if any proof is required, that the English 18th-century poets had no monopoly of the elegant, pithy epigram.*

*There seemed no good reason why the subjects of the poems selected should invariably be real people — is not Holy Willie as much a Scottish person as, say William Wallace? So Holy Willie's Prayer, perhaps the finest of Burns' satirical poems, will be found here, twinned with that other monstrous hypocrite, Sir David Lyndsay's Pardoner. And Wallace himself makes his first of two appearances in this book, in the ballad which describes quite a well-known, if not well-documented, incident in his early life.*

# The Braes o' Ballochmyle

The Catrine woods were yellow seen,
    The flowers decayed on Catrine lee,
Nae lav'rock sang on hillock green,
    But nature sickened on the ee.
Thro' faded groves Maria sang,
    Hersel in beauty's bloom the whyle,
And aye the wild-wood echoes rang,
    Fareweel the braes o' Ballochmyle.

Low in your wintry beds, ye flowers,
    Again ye'll flourish fresh and fair;
Ye birdies dumb, in withering bowers,
    Again ye'll charm the vocal air.
But here, alas! for me nae mair
    Shall birdie charm, or floweret smile;
Fareweel, the bonnie banks of Ayr,
    Fareweel, fareweel, sweet Ballochmyle.

Robert Burns (1759-1796)

# Amends to the Tailors and Shoemakers

Betuix twell houris and ellevin
I dremed ane angell came fra hevin
With plesand stevin sayand on hie,          *voice*
"Telyouris and sowtaris, blist be ye.

In hevin hie ordand is your place
Aboif all sanctis in grit solace,
Nixt God grittest in dignitie:
Tailyouris and sowtaris, blist be ye.

The caus to yow is nocht unkend:          *unknown*
That God mismakkis, ye do amend

Be craft and grit agilitie:
Tailyouris and sowtaris, blist be ye.

Sowtaris, with schone weill maid and meit
Ye mend the faltis of ill maid feit,
Quhairfoir to hevin your saulis will fle:
Telyouris and sowtaris, blist be ye.

Is nocht in all this fair a flyrok                    *deformed fellow*
That hes upoun his feit a wyrok,                      *corn*
Knowll tais, nor mowlis in no degrie,                 *knotted toes: chilblains*
Bot ye can hyd thame; blist be ye.

And ye tailyouris with weill maid clais
Can mend the werst maid man that gais
And mak him semely for to se:
Telyouris and sowtaris, blist be ye.

Thocht God mak ane misfassonit man
Ye can him all schaip new agane
And fassoun him bettir be sic thre:                   *three times as well*
Telyouris and sowtaris, blist be ye.

Thocht a man haif a brokin bak,
Haif he a gude telyour, quhatt rak,
That can it cuver with craftis slie:
Telyouris and sowtaris, blist be ye.

Off God grit kyndnes may ye clame,
That helpis his peple fra cruke and lame,
Supportand faltis with your supple:                   *help*
Tailyouris and sowtaris, blist be ye.

In erd ye kyth sic mirakillis heir,                   *show*
In hevin ye salbe sanctis full cleir,
Thocht ye be knavis in this cuntre:
Telyouris and sowtaris, blist be ye."

William Dunbar (c1460-c1521)

16

# ■ Epigram

*On Receiving a Present of an Orange from* Mrs G. L. *now*
*Countess of* Aboyne.

> Now, *Priam*'s Son, thou may'st be mute,
>> For I can blythly boast with thee;
> Thou to the Fairest gave the Fruit,
>> The Fairest gave the Fruit to me.

Allan Ramsay (1684-1758)

# ■ Satire on the Town Ladies

> Sum wyfis of the burrows-toun
> Sa wondir vane ar, and wantoun,               *wonderfully*
>> In warld thay watt not quhat to weir.        *know*
> On claythis thay wair mony a croun;           *spend*
>> And all for newfangilnes of geir.

> Thair bodyes bravelie thay atyir,
> Of carnall lust to eik the fyir;              *add to*
>> I fairlie quhy thai have na feir             *marvel*
> To gar men deime quhat thay desyre;           *make*
>> And all for newfangilnes of geir.

> Thair gouns ar coistlie, and trimlie traillis,
> Barrit with velvous, sleif, nek, and taillis;
>> And thair foirskirt of silkis seir           *many*
> Of fynest camroche thair fuksaillis;          *forecastles*
>> And all for newfangilnes of geir.

And of fyne silk thair furrit cloikis,
With hingand sleivis, lyk geill poikis;          *hanging: jelly bags*
  Na preiching will gar thame forbeir
To weir all thing that sinne provoikis;
  And all for newfangilnes of geir.

Thair wylecots man weill be hewit,               *petticoats must*
Broudirit richt braid, with pasmentis sewit:     *sewn with stripes*
  I trow, quha wald the matter speir,            *look into*
That thair gudmen had caus to rew it
  That evir thair wyfis weir sic geir.

Thair wovin hois of silk ar schawin,
Barrit abone with tasteis drawin;                *drawn head-pieces*
  With gartens of ane new maneir,
To gar thair courtlines be knawin;
  And all for newfangilnes of geir.

Sumtyme thay will beir up thair gown
To schaw thair wylecot hingeand down,
  And sumtyme bayth thay will upbeir
To schaw thair hois of blak or broun;
  And all for newfangilnes of geir.

Thair collars, carcats, and hals beidis,         *necklaces: throat beads*
With velvet hats heicht on thair heidis,         *high*
  Coirdit with gold lyik ane younkeir,           *youngster*
Brouderit about with goldin threidis;
  And all for newfangilnes of geir.

Thair schone of velvot, and thair muillis;       *sandals*
In kirk ar not content of stuillis,
  The sermon quhen thay sit to heir;
Bot caryis cuschingis lyik vaine fuillis;
  And all for newfangilnes of geir.

I mein of thame thair honour dreidis;            *lament*
Quhy sould thay nocht have honest weidis,

To thair estait doand effeir?                    *doing what is proper*
I mein of thame thair stait exceidis;
   And all for newfangilnes of geir.

For sumtymes wyfis sa grave hes bein,
Lyik giglets cled wald nocht be sein.            *girls*
   Of burgess wyfis thoch I speak heir
Think weill of all wemen I mein,
   On vaniteis that waistis geir.

Thay say wyfis ar so delicat
In feiding, feisting, and bankat,                *banquet*
   Sum not content ar with sic cheir       *demeanour*
As weill may suffice thair estait,
   For newfangilnes of cheir and geir.

And sum will spend mair, I heir say,
In spyce and droggis on ane day
   Than wald thair mothers in ane yeir;
Quhilk will gar monye pak decay,                 *fortune*
   Quhen thay sa vainlie waist thair geir.

Thairfoir, young wyfis speciallie,
Or all sic faultis hald yow frie,
   And moderatly to leif now leir          *learn*
In meit, and clayth accordinglie;
   And nocht sa vainlie waist your geir.

Use not to skift athort the gait,                *skip: street*
Nor na mum chairtis, air nor lait;               *playing cards*
   Be na dainser, nor this daingeir
Of yow be tane an ill consait
   That ye ar habill to waist geir.        *able*

Hant ay in honest cumpanie,                      *go around*
And all suspicious places flie;
   Lat never harlot cum yow neir,
That wald yow leid to leicherie,
   In houp to get thairfoir sum geir.

My counsall I geve generallie
To all wemen, quhat-evir thay be,
   This lesson for to quin per queir,    *learn by heart*
Syne keip it weill continuallie
   Better nor onye warldlie geir.

Leif, burgess men, or all be loist,    *leave off*
On your wyfis to mak sic cost,
   Quhilk may gar all your bairnis bleir:    *blame*
Scho that may not want wyne and roist    *she*
   Is abill for to waist sum geir.    *money*

Betwene thame and nobillis of blude
Na difference bot ane velvous huid!
   Thair camroche curcheis ar als deir;    *handkerchiefs*
Thair uther claythis ar als guid;
   And thai als costlie in uther geir.

Bot, wald grit ladyis tak gud heid
To thair honour, and find remeid,
   Thai suld thole na sic wyfis to weir,
Lyk lordis wyfis, ladyis weid,
   As dames of honour in thair geir.

I speik for na despyt trewlie,
(My-self am nocht of faultis frie),
   Bot that ye sould nocht perseveir
Into sic folische vanitie
   For na newfangilnes of geir.

Of burgess wyfis thoch I speik plaine,
Sum landwart ladyis ar als vain,    *country*
   As be thair cleithing may appeir;
Werand gayer nor thame may gain —    *wearing*
   On ouir vaine claythis waistand geir.    *over*

Sir Richard Maitland (1496-1586)

# To a Lady
*Who was looking up the text during sermon.*

Fair maid, you need not take the hint,
    Nor idle texts pursue:
'Twas *guilty sinners* that he meant —
    Not *angels* such as you!

Robert Burns (1759-1796)

# Sir William Wallace

Wou'd ye hear of William Wallace,
    And seek him as he goes,
Into the land of Lanark,
    Amang his mortal foes?

There were fifteen English sogers
    Unto his ladye came,
Said — "Gi'e us William Wallace,
    That we may have him slain.

"Wou'd ye gi'e William Wallace,
    That we may have him slain?
And ye'se be wedded to a lord,
    The best in Christendeem."

"This very night, at seven,
    Brave Wallace will come in,
And he'll come to my chamber door,
    Without or dread or din."

The fifteen English sogers
    Around the house did wait;
And four brave Southron foragers
    Stood hie upon the gait.

That very night, at seven,
   Brave Wallace he came in,
And he came to his ladye's bow'r
   Withouten dread or din.

When she beheld brave Wallace,
   And stared him in the face —
"Ohon, alas!" said that ladye,
   "This is a woeful case.

"For I this night have sold you,
   This night you must be ta'en;
And I'm to be wedded to a lord,
   The best in Christendeem."

"Do you repent," said Wallace,
   "The ill you've done to me?"
"Ay, that I do," said that ladye,
   "And will do till I dee."

"Ay, that I do," said that ladye,
   "And will do ever still;
And for the ill I've done to you,
   Let me burn upon a hill."

"Now, God forfend," says brave Wallace,
   "I should be so unkind;
Whatever I am to Scotland's faes,
   I'm aye a woman's friend.

"Will ye gi'e me your gown, your gown,
   Your gown but and your kirtle,
"Your petticoat of bonnie brown,
   And belt about my middle?

"I'll take a pitcher in ilka hand,
   And do me to the well;
They'll think I'm one of your maidens,
   Or think it is yoursel'."

She has gi'en him her gown, her gown,
    Her petticoat and kirtle;
Her broadest belt with silver clasps,
    To bind about his middle.

Then he ga'e her a loving kiss,
    The tear dropp'd frae his e'e;
Says — "Fare ye well for evermair,
    Your face I'll nae mair see."

He's ta'en a pitcher in ilka hand,
    And done him to the well;
They thought him one of her maidens,
    They kenn'd 'twas not hersel'.

Said one of the Southron foragers, —
    "See ye yon lusty dame?
I wou'd nae gi'e meikle to thee, neebor,
    To bring her back again."

Then all the Southrons follow'd him,
    They follow'd him all four;
But he has drawn his trusty brand,
    And slain them pair by pair.

# Holy Willie's Prayer

O Thou, wha in the Heavens dost dwell,
Wha, as it pleases best thysel',
Sends ane to heaven and ten to hell,
   A' for thy glory,
And no for ony guid or ill
   They've done afore thee!

I bless and praise thy matchless might,
Whan thousands thou hast left in night,
That I am here afore thy sight,
   For gifts an' grace
A burnin' an' a shinin' light,
   To a' this place.

What was I, or my generation,
That I should get sic exaltation?
I, wha deserve most just damnation,
   For broken laws,
Sax thousand years 'fore my creation,
   Thro' Adam's cause.

When frae my mither's womb I fell,
Thou might hae plunged me in hell,
To gnash my gums, to weep and wail,
   In burnin' lakes,
Where damned devils roar and yell,
   Chain'd to their stakes;

Yet I am here a chosen sample,
To show thy grace is great and ample;
I'm here a pillar in thy temple,
   Strong as a rock,
A guide, a buckler, an example
   To a' thy flock.

O Lord, thou kens what zeal I bear,
When drinkers drink, and swearers swear,
And singin' there and dancin' here,
　　Wi' great an' sma':
For I am keepit by thy fear
　　Free frae them a'.


But yet, O Lord! confess I must
At times I'm fash'd wi' fleshy lust;
An' sometimes too, in warldly trust,
　　Vile self gets in;
But thou remembers we are dust,
　　Defil'd in sin.


O Lord! yestreen, thou kens, wi' Meg —
Thy pardon I sincerely beg;
O! may't ne'er be a livin' plague
　　To my dishonour,
An' I'll ne'er lift a lawless leg
　　Again upon her.


Besides I farther maun allow,
Wi' Lizzie's lass, three times I trow —
But, Lord, that Friday I was fou,
　　When I cam near her,
Or else thou kens thy servant true
　　Wad never steer her.


May be thou lets this fleshy thorn
Beset thy servant e'en and morn
Lest he owre high and proud should turn,
　　That he's sae gifted;
If sae, thy hand maun e'en be borne,
　　Until thou lift it.

Lord, bless thy chosen in this place,
For here thou hast a chosen race;
But God confound their stubborn face,
    And blast their name,
Wha bring thy elders to disgrace
    An' public shame.


Lord, mind Gawn Hamilton's deserts,
He drinks, an' swears, an' plays at cartes,
Yet has sae mony takin' arts
    Wi' grit an' sma',
Frae God's ain priest the people's hearts
    He steals awa'.


An' when we chasten'd him therefor,
Thou kens how he bred sic a splore
As set the warld in a roar
    O' laughin' at us;
Curse thou his basket and his store,
    Kail and potatoes.


Lord, hear my earnest cry an' pray'r,
Against that presbyt'ry o' Ayr;
Thy strong right hand, Lord, make it bare
    Upo' their heads;
Lord, weigh it down, and dinna spare,
    For their misdeeds.


O Lord my God, that glib-tongu'd Aiken,
My very heart and soul are quakin',
To think how we stood sweatin', shakin',
    An' piss'd wi' dread,
While he, wi' hingin' lips and snakin',
    Held up his head.

Lord, in the day of vengeance try him;
Lord, visit them wha did employ him,
And pass not in thy mercy by them,
    Nor hear their pray'r:
But, for thy people's sake, destroy them,
    And dinna spare.


But, Lord, remember me and mine
Wi' mercies temp'ral and divine,
That I for gear and grace may shine
    Excell'd by nane,
And a' the glory shall be thine,
    Amen, Amen!

Robert Burns (1759-1796)

# *From* A Satire of the Three Estates

PARDONER
*Bona dies, Bona dies.*
Devoit peopill, gude day I say yow.
Now tarie ane lytill quhyll I pray yow,
    Till I be with yow knawin:
Wait ye weill how I am namit?                    *know*
Ane nobill man and vndefamit
    Gif all the suith war schawin.                *truth*
I am sir Robert Rome-raker,
Ane perfite publike pardoner,
    Admittit be the Paip.
Sirs I sall schaw yow for my wage
My pardons and my pilgramage,
    Quhilk ye sall se and graip.
I giue to the deuill with gude intent,
This vnsell wickit New-testament,              *worthless*
    With them that it translaitit:

Sen layik men knew the veritie,                    *since*
Pardoners gets no charitie,
   Without that thay debait it
Amang the wiues with wrinks and wyles,
As all my marrowis men begyles               *fellow*
   With our fair fals flattrie:
Yea all the crafts I ken perqueir,               *off hand*
As I was teichit be ane Freir,
   Callit Hypocrisie.
Bot now allace, our greit abusioun
Is cleirlie knawin till our confusioun,
   That we may sair repent:
Of all credence now I am quyte,
For ilk man halds me at dispyte,
   That reids the New-test'ment.
Duill fell the braine that hes it wrocht,
Sa fall them that the Buik hame brocht:
   Als I pray to the Rude
That Martin Luther that fals loun,
Black Bullinger and Melancthoun,
   Had bene smorde in their cude.      *smothered: baptismal robe*
Be him that buir the crowne of thorne,
I wald Sanct Paull had neuer bene borne,
   And als I wald his buiks
War never red into the kirk,
Bot amangs freirs into the mirk,               *dark*
   Or riuen amang ruiks.

*Heir sall he lay doun his geir vpon ane buird*

My patent pardouns ye may se,
Cum fra the Caue of Tartarie,
   Weill seald with oster-schellis.
Thocht ye haue na contritioun,
Ye sall haue full remissioun,
   With help of Buiks and bellis.
Heir is ane relict lang and braid,
Of fine Macoull the richt chaft blaid,
   With teith and al togidder:

Of Collings cow heir is ane horne;
For eating of Makconnals corne,
   Was slaine into Baquhidder.
Heir is ane coird baith great and lang,
Quhilk hangit Johne the Armistrang,
   Of gude hemp soft and sound:
Gude halie peopill I stand for'd,
Quha ever beis hangit with this cord,
   Neids never to be dround.
The culum of Sanct Brydis kow,       *tail*
The gruntill of Sanct Antonis sow,    *snout*
   Quhilk buir his haly bell:
Quha ever he be heiris this bell clinck
Gif me ane ducat for till drink,
   He sall never gang to hell,
Without he be of Baliell borne.
Maisters trow ye that this be scorne?
   Cum win this pardoun, cum.
Quha luifis thair wyfis nocht with thair hart,
I haue power them for till part.
   Me think yow deif and dum.
Hes naine of yow curst wickit wyfis,
That halds yow into sturt and stryfis?    *annoyance*
   Cum tak my dispensatioun:
Of that cummer I sall mak yow quyte,    *shrew*
Howbeit your selfis be in the wyte,    *blame*
   And mak ane fals narratioun.
Cum win the pardoun, now let se,
For meill, for malt or for monie,
   For cok, hen, guse or gryse.    *pig*
Of relicts heir I haue ane hunder.
Quhy cum ye nocht? This is ane wonder.
   I trow ye be nocht wyse.

Sir David Lyndsay (c1486-1555)

My delight it was to rise
With the early morning skies,
 All aglow,
And to brush the dewy height
Where the deer in airy state
 Wont to go;
At least a hundred brace
Of the lofty-antlered race,
When they left their sleeping-place,
 Light and gay;
When they stood in trim array,
And with low deep-breasted cry,
Flung their breath into the sky,
 From the brae:
When the hind, the pretty fool,
Would be rolling in the pool
 At her will;
Or the stag in gallant pride,
Would be strutting at the side
Of his haughty-headed bride,
 On the hill.
And sweeter to my ear
Is the concert of the deer
 In their roaring,
Than when Erin from her lyre
Warmest strains of Celtic fire
 May be pouring;
And no organ sends a roll
So delightsome to my soul,
As the branchy-crested race,
When they quicken their proud pace
And bellow in the face
 Of Ben Dorain.
O what joy to view the stag
When he rises 'neath the crag,
And from the depth of hollow chest
Sends his bell across the waste,

While he tosses high his crest,
    Proudly scorning.
And from milder throat the hind,
Lows an answer to his mind,
With the younglings of her kind
    In the morning;
With her vivid swelling eye,
While her antlered lord is nigh,
She sweeps both earth and sky,
    Far away;
And beneath her eyebrow grey
Lifts her lid to greet the day,
And to guide her turfy way
    O'er the brae.
O how lightsome in her tread,
When she gaily goes ahead
O'er the green and mossy bed
    Of the rills;
When she leaps with such a grace
You will own her pretty pace
Ne'er was hindmost in the race,
    When she wills;
Or when with sudden start
She defies the hunter's art,
And is vanished like a dart
    O'er the hills!
And her food full well she knows,
In the forest where she goes,
Where the rough old pasture grows
    To her mind.
Stiff grass of virtue rare,
Glossy fatness to prepare,
'Neath her coat of shining hair,
    To the hind;
And for drink she hath the well,
Where the water-cresses dwell,
Far sweeter to her taste,
In the freshness of the waste,
    Than sweet wine;

The blushing daisy-tips
Are a dainty to her lips,
As the nodding grass she clips,
    Very fine;
St John's wort too she knows,
And where the sweet primrose
And the spotted orchis grows,
    She will dine.
With such food and drink, I ween,
You will never find them lean,
But girt with pith and power,
To stand stoutly in the hour
    Of distress;
And though laden on the back
With weighty fat no lack,
With well-compacted limb
They will wear it light and trim,
    Like a dress.
O how pleasant 'twas to see
How happy they would be,
When they gathered all together
To their home upon the heather,
    In the gloaming!
At the bottom of the hill
They were safe from touch of ill,
In their nook of shelter tight,
When they rested for the night
    From their roaming.
What though the nights were long,
And the winds were sharp and strong,
    In their roaring,
Wrapt in thick fur of the red,
Where the moor is widely spread,
Here they made their turfy bed,
And their sleep was sweet and sound,
With no wish beyond the bound
    Of Ben Dorain.

Duncan Ban MacIntyre (1724-1812)
Translated from the Gaelic
by John Stuart Blackie

# The Daft Days

Now mirk December's dowie face
Glowrs owre the rigs wi' sour grimace,
While, thro his *minimum* o' space
    The bleer-e'ed sun,
Wi' blinkin light and stealin' pace,
    His race doth run.

Frae naked groves nae birdie sings;
To shepherd's pipe nae hillock rings;
The breeze nae od'rous flavour brings,
    Frae Borean cave;
And dwynin Nature droops her wings,
    Wi' visage grave.

Mankind but scanty pleasure glean
Frae snawy hill or barren plain,
Whan Winter, 'midst his nippin' train,
    Wi' frozen spear,
Sends drift owre a' his bleak domain,
    And guides the weir.

Auld Reikie! thou'rt the canty hole;
A bield for mony a cauldrife soul,
Wha snugly at thine ingle loll,
    Baith warm and couth;
While round they gar the bicker roll,
    To weet their mouth.

Whan merry Yule-day comes, I trow,
You'll scantlins find a hungry mou;
Sma' are our cares, our stamacks fou
    O' gusty gear,
And kickshaws, strangers to our view
    Sin' fairn-year.

Ye browster wives! now busk ye braw,
And fling your sorrows far awa;
Then, come and gie's the tither blaw
    O' reaming ale,
Mair precious than the Well o' Spa,
    Our hearts to heal.

Then, tho' at odds wi' a' the warl',
Amang oursels we'll never quarrel;
Tho' Discord gie a canker'd snarl,
    To spoil our glee,
As lang's there's pith into the barrel,
    We'll drink and gree.

Fiddlers! your pins in temper fix,
And roset weel your fiddlesticks;
But banish vile Italian tricks
    Frae out your quorum;
Nor fortes wi' pianos mix; —
    Gie's Tullochgorum.

For nought can cheer the heart sae weel,
As can a canty Highland reel;
It even vivifies the heel
    To skip and dance:
Lifeless is he wha canna feel
  `  Its influence.

Let mirth abound; let social cheer
Invest the dawnin' o' the year;
Let blithsome Innocence appear,
    To crown our joy:
Nor Envy, wi' sarcastic sneer,
    Our bliss destroy.

And thou, great god of *Aquavitae!*
Wha sways the empire o' this city; —
Whan fou, we're sometimes capernoity; —
   Be thou prepar'd
To hedge us frae that black banditti,
   The City Guard.

Robert Fergusson (1750-1774)

# In Orkney

Vpon the vtmost corners of the warld,
and on the borders of this massiue round,
quhaire fates and fortoune hither hes me harld,
I doe deplore my greiffs vpon this ground;
and seing roring seis from roks rebound
by ebbs and streames of contrair routing tyds,
and phebus chariot in there wawes ly dround,
quha equallye now night and day devyds,
I cal to mynde the storms my thoughts abyds,
which euer wax and never dois decress,
for nights of dole dayes Ioys ay euer hyds,
and in there vayle doith al my weill suppress:
   so this I see, quhaire euer I remove,
   I chainge bot sees, but can not chainge my love.

William Fowler (1560-1612)

# ■ Banishment

Alone on the hill-top, sadly and silently,
Downward on Islay and over the sea,
I look, and I wonder how time hath deceived me —
A stranger in Scarba, who ne'er thought to be.

Ne'er thought it, my island, where rest the deep dark shade
The grand mossy mountains for ages have made;
God bless thee! and prosper thy chief of the sharp blade;
All over these islands his fame never fade!

Never fade it, Sir Norman! for well 'tis the right
Of thy name to win credit in counsel or fight —
By wisdom, by shrewdness, by spirit, by might,
By manliness, courage, by daring, by sleight.

In counsel or fight, thy kindred know these should be thine —
Branch of Lochlin's wide-ruling and king-bearing line!
And in Erin they know it, far over the brine;
No Earl would in Albin thy friendship decline.

Mary Macleod (1569-1674)
Translated from the Gaelic
by Rev. Thomas Pattison

# Logan Braes

By Logan's streams that rin sae deep
Fu' aft, wi' glee, I've herded sheep —
I've herded sheep, or gathered slaes
Wi' my dear lad on Logan Braes.
But wae's my heart, thae days are gane,
And fu' o' grief, I herd my lane,
While my dear lad maun face his faes,
Far, far frae me and Logan Braes.

Nae mair, at Logan Kirk, will he,
Atween the preachings, meet wi' me —
Meet wi' me, or, when it's mirk,
Convoy me hame frae Logan Kirk.
I weel may sing, thae days are gane;
Frae kirk and fair I come alane,
While my dear lad maun face his faes,
Far, far frae me and Logan Braes.

At e'en, when hope amaist is gane,
I dander dowie and forlane,
Or sit beneath the trysting tree,
Where first he spak' o' love to me.
O! could I see thae days again,
My lover skaithless and my ain,
Revered by friends, and far frae faes,
We'd live in bliss on Logan Braes.

John Mayne (1759-1836)

# The Braes o' Menstrie

O Alva hills is bonny,
   Dalcoutry hills is fair;
But to think on the braes o' Menstrie,
It maks my heart fu' sair.

# It is Time for Me to Go up into the House of Paradise

In Iona of my heart, Iona of my love
Instead of monks' voices shall be lowing of cattle;
But ere the world shall come to an end
Iona shall be as it was.

Traditional
Translated from the Gaelic

# Kings and Queens

*The verse about the death by accident in 1286 of Alexander III with which this section opens is the earliest surviving Scottish poem. Almost thirty years of "perplexity" followed, which were only ended when Robert I (The Bruce) took the throne and swept away the English army at Bannockburn in 1314. The intervening years had seen the rise, success and ignominious execution by Edward I of William Wallace, who had been victorious at Stirling Bridge in 1297. After that battle he led his troops down into England. The Queen, in Blind Harry's epic about Wallace, is Eleanor of Castile, wife of Edward I, but the meeting is apocryphal, as in fact Wallace turned back at Newcastle. However, the extract here provides further literary evidence of Wallace's prowess as a ladies' man.*

*James I had the singular misfortune to be captured at sea by the English on the day his father Robert III died. He remained a prisoner for the first 18 years of his reign, though he was given the best education the English court could provide. During this time he wrote The Kingis Quair (The Book of the King), surely the finest poem ever composed by a reigning monarch. That argumentative and often morose cleric, William Dunbar, was a member of the court of James IV, to whom he addressed a number of querulous poems on the subject of his pension. That quoted here also illustrates the richness as well as the corruption of the Court during what is regarded as a golden age in Scottish history. Sir David Lyndsay was Lyon King at Arms in the reign of James V, but it must have been in his former role as tutor to the young King that he addressed to him several admonitory poems, of which the one here is a fairly mild example. James V died in 1542 in a miserable fit of depression only a few days after the birth of his only surviving legitimate child, Mary, and having delivered himself of the deathbed prophecy about the Stewart succession to the throne, "It came wi' a lass, and it'll gang wi' a lass," or words, according to different chroniclers, to that effect.*

*Mary Queen of Scots, having spent all her formative years in France as future wife, and then wife, of the boy-king Francis II, returned after his death to Scotland in 1562, to be welcomed as Queen, as Alexander Scott's* poem records. Though in some respects Mary proved herself a good ruler, it was her penchant for selecting unsuitable husbands that caused her to lose her crown and, ultimately, her head. The King in the ballad <u>The Queen's Marie</u> is her cousin, Lord Darnley, whom she married in 1565. She did have four Maries, her comtemporaries chosen from prominent Scottish families to accompany her to France. The fervent Protestant cleric John Knox records, with some relish, how one of Mary's French waiting-women and her lover, the Queen's apothecary, had been hanged after their bastard child had been found dead. This is the probable provenance of the ballad, with the apothecary becoming Darnley, about whose behaviour, even with her own attendants, Mary complained. After marrying the Earl of Bothwell, the probable murderer of Darnley, Mary was forced to abdicate in favour of her baby son, James VI (later to be also James I of England).

James, in spite of his ungainly appearance and disgusting table manners, was a keen sportsman and a fair scholar, as his sonnet suggests. He married the Danish Princess Anne and their eldest child, Henry, Prince of Wales, was born in 1594. Robert Ayton was cordially received at court in London when he went there in 1603. The cordiality was repaid by poems of which two are quoted here. Ayton was knighted in 1612, the year Prince Henry died. William Alexander was tutor to the Prince and in that capacity would have addressed to him the "exhortation". His poem, then, to the future Charles I must therefore rank as what the Scots call "sooking". So Charles was not born to be King, and Montrose's lines on his subsequent execution at the hands of the English Parliament reflect the horror that many Scots felt.

# "When Alysandyr our King was Dede"

When Alysandyr our King was dede
   That Scotland led in luve and le,     *peace*
Away was sons of ale and brede,     *abundance*
   Of wine and wax, of gamyn and gle;
Our gold was changyd into lede.
   Christ born into Virginitie
Succour Scotland and remede     *redeem*
   That stad is in perplexytie.

# *From* Sir William Wallace

Out off the south thai saw quhar at the queyn
Towart the ost come ridand sobyrly,                    *host*
And fyfty ladyis, was in hyr cumpany,
Waillyt off wit and demyt off renoun;                  *chosen: judged*
Sum wedowis war and sum off Religioun;
And vii preistis that entrit war in age.
Wallace to sic did neuir gret owtrage
Bot gyff till him thai maid a gret offens.
Thus prochyt thai on towart thar presens.
At the palyoun quhar thai the lyoun saw               *pavilion*
To ground thai lycht and syne on kneis can faw;       *then*
Prayand for pece thai cry with petous cher.           *aspect*
Erll Malcom said, "Our chyftayn is nocht her."
He bad hyr rys and said it was nocht rycht,
A queyn on kneis till ony lavar wycht.                 *lowly*
Wp by the hand the gud Erll has hyr tayn.
Atour the bent to Wallace ar thai gayn.               *across the field*
Quhen scho him saw scho wald haiff knelyt doun.
In armys sone he caucht this queyn with croun
And kyssyt hyr with-outyn wordis mor.
Sa dyd he neuir to na Sotheron befor.
"Madem," he said, "rycht welcum mot ye be.
How plesis yow our ostyng for to se?"
"Rycht weyll," scho said, "off frendschip haiff we neid.
God grant ye wald off our nesis to speid.
Suffyr we mon suppos it lik ws ill,
Bot trastis weyll it is contrar our will."             *believe*
"Ye sall remayn. With this lord I mon gang.
Fra your presens we sall nocht tary lang."

Blind Harry (c1440-c1492)

# Scots Wha Hae

ROBERT BRUCE'S ADDRESS TO HIS ARMY, BEFORE THE
BATTLE OF BANNOCKBURN.

Scots, wha hae wi' Wallace bled,
Scots, wham Bruce has aften led,
Welcome to your gory bed,
   Or to victorie.

Now's the day, and now's the hour;
See the front o' battle lour!
See approach proud Edward's power —
   Chains and slaverie!

Wha will be a traitor knave?
Wha can fill a coward's grave?
Wha sae base as be a slave?
   Let him turn and flee!

Wha for Scotland's King and law
Freedom's sword will strongly draw,
Freeman stand, or freeman fa'?
   Let him follow me!

By oppression's woes and pains!
By your sons in servile chains!
We will drain our dearest veins,
   But they shall be free!

Lay the proud usurpers low!
Tyrants fall in every foe!
Liberty's in every blow!
   Let us do or die!

Robert Burns (1759-1796)

# *From* The Kingis Quair

| | |
|---|---|
| Quhare in a lusty plane tuke I my way, | *pleasant* |
| Endlang a ryuer plesant to behold, | *beside* |
| Enbroudin all with fresche flouris gay, | |
| Quhare throu the grauel bryght as ony gold | |
| The cristall water ran so clere and cold, | |
| That in myn ere maid contynualy | |
| A maner soun, mellit with armony, | *mingled* |

| | |
|---|---|
| That full of lytill fischis by the brym | |
| Now here now there with bakkis blewe as lede | |
| Lap and playit, and in a rout can swym | |
| So prattily, and dressit tham to sprede | |
| Thair curall fynnis as the ruby rede, | |
| That in the sonne on thair scalis bryght | |
| As gesserant ay glitterit in my sight. | *armour* |

| | |
|---|---|
| And by this ilke ryuer syde alawe | *lower down* |
| Ane hye-way fand I like to bene, | |
| On quhich on euery syde a long rawe | |
| Of treis saw I, full of leuis grene, | |
| That full of fruyte delitable were to sene. | |
| And also, as it come vnto my mynd, | |
| Of bestis sawe I mony diuerse kynd: | |

| | |
|---|---|
| The lyoun king and his fere lyonesse, | |
| The pantere like vnto the smaragdyne, | *emerald* |
| The lytill squerell full of besynesse, | |
| The slawe ase, the druggar, beste of pyne, | *drudger* |
| The nyce ape, the werely porpapyne, | *foolish: warlike* |
| The percyng lynx, the lufare vnicorne | *sharp-sighted: lover* |
| That voidis venym with his euour horne. | *makes harmless* |

There saw I dresse him new out of haunt
The fery tiger full of felonye;
The dromydare, the standar oliphant,                    *jointless*
The wyly fox, the wedowis inemye;
The clymbare gayte, the elk for alblastrye,             *clambering: crossbows*
The herknere bore, the holsum grey for hortis,          *listening: badger: wounds*
The hair also that oft gooth to the wortis;             *cabbage patch*

The bugill drawar by his hornis grete,                  *wild ox*
The martrik sable, the foynyee, and mony mo;            *marten: beach marten: many*
The chalk-quhite`ermyn tippit as the iete,              *jet*
The riall hert, the conyng, and the ro,                 *royal: coney*
The wolf that of the murthir noght say "ho",
The lesty beuer and the ravin bare,                     *skilful*
For chamelot the camel full of hare,                    *costly fabric*

With mony anothir beste diuerse and strange
That cummyth noght as now vnto my mynd.

James I (1394-1437)

# Remonstrance to the King

Schir, ye have mony servitouris
And officiaris of dyvers curis;                    *functions*
Kirkmen, courtmen, and craftismen fyne,
Doctouris in jure and medicyne,
Divinouris, rethoris, and philosophouris,          *speech-writers*
Astrologis, artistis, and oratouris,
Men of armes and vailyeand knychtis,
And mony uther gudlie wichtis;                     *fellows*
Musicianis, menstralis, and mirrie singaris,
Chevalouris, cawandaris, and flingaris,
Cunyouris, carvouris, and carpentaris,             *coiners*
Beildaris of barkis and ballingaris,               *ships: boats*
Masounis lyand upon the land,                      *building*
And schipwrichtis hewand upone the strand,
Glasing wrichtis, goldsmythis, and lapidaris,
Pryntouris, payntouris, and potingaris;            *apothecaries*
And all of thair craft cunning
And all at anis lawboring,
Quhilk pleisand ar and honorable
And to your hienes profitable,
And richt convenient for to be
With your hie regale majestie,
Deserving of your grace most ding                  *worthy*
Bayth thank, rewarde, and cherissing.
    And thocht that I amang the laif               *rest*
Unworthy be ane place to have
Or in thair nummer to be tald;
Als lang in mynd my wark sall hald,
Als haill in everie circumstance,                  *whole*
In forme, in mater, and substance,
But wering or consumptioun,
Roust, canker or corruptioun,
As ony of thair werkis all,
Suppois that my rewarde be small.                  *although*
    Bot ye sa gracious ar and meik
That on your hienes followis eik
Ane uthir sort, more miserabill,

Thocht thai be nocht sa profitable: *though*
Fenyeouris, fleichouris, and flatteraris, *pretenders: fawners*
Cryaris, craikaris, and clatteraris, *bawlers: boasters: gossips*
Soukaris, groukaris, gledaris, gunnaris,
Monsouris of France, gud clarat cunnaris, *connoisseurs of claret*
Innopportoun askaris of Yrland kynd,
And meit revaris lyk out of mynd, *meat-thieves*
Scaffaris and scamleris in the nuke, *spongers: parasites: corner*
And hall huntaris of draik and duik, *duck*
Thrimlaris and thristaris as thay war woid, *jostlers: thrusters: mad*
Kokenis, and kennis na man of gude, *rascals*
Schulderaris and schowaris that hes no schame, *pushers: shovers*
And to no cunning that can clame,
And can non uthir craft nor curis
Bot to mak thrang, schir, in your duris, *doors*
And rusche in quhair thay counsale heir,
And will at na man nurtir leyr: *manners: learn*
In quintiscence eik ingynouris joly *alchemists*
That far can multiplie in folie,
Fantastik fulis bayth fals and gredy,
Off toung untrew and hand evill diedie: *prone to evil deeds*
Few dar of all this last additioun
Cum in tolbuyth without remissioun.

And thocht this nobill cunning sort
Quhom of befoir I did report
Rewardit be, it war bot ressoun,
Thairat suld no man mak enchessoun; *objection*
Bot quhen the uther fulis nyce *wanton fools*
That feistit at Cokelbeis gryce
Ar all rewardit, and nocht I,
Than on this fals world I cry, fy:
My hart neir bristis than for teyne, *bursts: anger*
Quhilk may nocht suffer nor sustene
So grit abusioun for to se
Daylie in court befoir myn e.

And yit more panence wald I have,
Had I rewarde amang the laif:
It wald me sumthing satisfie
And les of my malancolie,
And gar me mony falt ouerse *overlook*

47

That now is brayd befoir myn e:
My mind so fer is set to flyt
That of nocht ellis I can endyt,                    *write*
For owther man my hart to breik
Or with my pen I man me wreik;
And sen the tane most nedis be,                     *that one*
In to malancolie to de
Or lat the vennim ische all out,                    *pour*
Be war, anone, for it will spout,
Gif that the tryackill cum nocht tyt               *antidote: quickly*
To swage the swalme of my despyt.                  *swelling: indignation*

William Dunbar (c1460-c1555)

# An Exhortation to His Grace the King

Schir, sen that God, of his preordinance,
Haith grantit thee to have the governance
   Of his peple, and create thee ane Kyng;
Faill nocht to prent in thy rememberance,
That he wyll nocht excuse thyne ignorance,
   Geve thow be rekles, in thy governyng:
   Quharefor, dress thee, above all uther thyng,
Of his lawis to keip the observance,
   And thou schaip lang in Royaltie to ryng.       *reign*

Thank Hym that hes commandit dame Nature
To prent thee of so plesand portrature:
   Hir gyftis may be cleirly on thee knawin.
Tyll dame Fortune thow nedis no procurature;
For scho hes lairglie kyith on thee hir cure,       *bestowed: care*
   Hir gratytude sche hes unto thee schawin:
   And, sen that thow mon scheir as thow hes sawin,   *reap*
Have all thy hope in God, thy Creature,
   And aske Hym grace, that thow may be his awin.

And syne, considder thy vocatioun,
That for to have the gubernatioun
   Of this Kynrik, thow art predestinate.
Thow may weill wyt, be trew narratioun,       *know*
Quhat sorrow, and quhat trubulatioun,
   Haith bene in this pure realme infortunate.
   Now conforte thame that hes bene desolate;
And of thy peple have compassioun,
   Sen thow be God art so preordinate.

Tak manlie curage, and leif thyne insolence,
And use counsale of nobyll dame Prudence;
   Founde thee firmelie on Faith, and Fortytude;
Drawe to thy courte Justice and Temperance;
And to the Commounweill have attendance.

And also, I beseik thy Celsitude,
Hait vicious men, and lufe thame that ar gude;
And ilke flattrer thou fleme frome thy presence,          *drive away*
    And fals reporte out of thy Courte exclude.

Do equale justice boith to gret and small;
And be exampyll to thy peple all,
    Exerceng verteous deidis honorabyll.
Be nocht ane wrache, for oucht that may befall:
To that unhappy vice and thow be thrall,
    Tyll all men thow sall be abhominabyll.
    Kyngis nor knychtis ar never convenabyll
To rewle peple, be thay nocht lyberall:
    Was never yit na wrache to honour habyll.          *wretch: qualified*

And tak exempyll of the wracheit endyng
Quhilk maid Mydas of Trace, the mychtie king,
    That to his Goddis maid invocatioun
Throw gredines, that all substanciall thing
That ever he twycheit suld turne, but taryying,          *touched: at once*
    In to fyne gold: he gat his supplicatioun;
    All that he twychit, but delatioun,          *without delay*
Turnit in gold, boith meit, drynk, and clethyng;
    And deit of hounger, but recreatioun.

Als, I beseik thy Majestie serene,
Frome lychorie thow keip thy body clene;
    Taist never that intoxicat poysoun:
Frome that unhappy sensuall syn abstene,
Tyll that thow get ane lusty, plesand Quene:
    Than tak thy plesour, with my benesoun.
    Tak tent how prydful Tarquyne tynt his croun,          *lost*
For the deforsyng of Lucres, the schene,          *lovely*
    And was depryvit, and baneist Romis toun.

And, in dispyit of his lycherous levyng,
The Romanis wald be subject to no kyng,
   Mony lang yeir, as storyis doith recorde,
Tyll Julyus, throw verteous governyng
And princelie curage, gane on thame to ryng,
   And, chosin of Romanis, Empriour and lord.
   Quharfor, my Soverane, in to thy mynd remord,     *remember*
That vicious lyfe makis oft ane evyll endyng,
   Without it be throw speciall grace restord.

And geve thow wald thy fame, and honour, grew,
Use counsall of thy prudent Lordis trew,
   And see thow nocht presumpteouslie pretend
Thy awin perticulare weill for tyll ensew:     *benefit*
Wyrk with counsall, so sall thou never rew.
   Remember of thy freindis the fatell end,
   Quhilks to gude counsall wald not condescend,
Tyll bitter deith, allace! did thame persew.
   Frome sic unhap, I pray God thee defend!

And fynalie, remember thow mon dee,
And suddanlie pass of this mortall see:
   And art nocht sicker of thy lyfe two houris;
Sen thare is none frome that sentence may flee,
Kyng, Quene, or Knycht, of lawe estait, nor hie,
   Bot all mon thole of Deith the bitter schouris:
   Quhar bene thay gone, thir Papis and Empriouris?
Bene thay nocht dede? so sall it fair on thee:
   Is no remeid, strenth, ryches, nor honouris.

   And so, for conclusioun,
   Mak our provisioun,
   To get the infusioun
     Of His hie grace:
   Quhilk bled, with effusioun,
   With scorne and derisioun,
   And deit, with confusion,
     Confirmand our peace.    Amen!

Sir David Lyndsay (c1486-1555)

# *From* A New Year Gift to the Queen Mary when she first came home, 1562

Welcum, illustrat Ladye, and oure Quene!
Welcum, oure lyone with the Floure-delyce!
Welcum, oure thrissill with the Lorane grene!
Welcum, oure rubent roiss upoun the ryce!                    *stem*
Welcum, oure jem and joyfull genetryce!
Welcum, oure beill of Albion to beir!                        *protection: bear*
Welcum, oure plesand Princes maist of pryce!
God gif thee grace aganis this guid new yeir.                *for*

This guid new yeir, we hoip, with grace of God,
Salbe of peax, tranquillitie, and rest;
This yeir sall rycht and ressone rewle the rod,
Quhilk sa lang seasoun has bene soir supprest;
This yeir ferme fayth sall frelie be confest,
And all erronius questionis put areir;
To laboure that this lyfe amang us lest                      *lasts*
God gif thee grace aganis this guid new yeir.

Heirfore addres thee dewlie to decoir                        *adorn*
And rewle thy regne with hie magnificence;
Begin at God to gar sett furth his gloir,
And of his gospell gett experience;
Caus his trew Kirk be had in reverence;
So sall thy name and fame spred far and neir:
Now, this thy dett to do with diligence,                     *duty*
God gif thee grace aganis this guid new yeir.

Alexander Scott (c1515-1583)

# The Queen's Marie

Marie Hamilton's to the kirk gane,
　　With ribbons in her hair;
The King thought mair of Marie Hamilton,
　　Than ony that were there.

Marie Hamilton's to the kirk gane,
　　With ribbons on her breast;
The King thought mair of Marie Hamilton,
　　Than he listen'd to the priest.

Marie Hamilton's to the kirk gane,
　　With gloves upon her hands;
The King thought mair of Marie Hamilton,
　　Than the Queen and all her lands.

She hadna been about the King's court
　　A month but barely one,
Till she was beloved by all the King's court,
　　And the King the only man.

She hadna been about the King's court
　　A month but barely three,
Till frae the King's court Marie Hamilton,
　　Marie Hamilton durstna be.

The King is to the Abbey gane,
　　To pull the Abbey tree,
To scale the babe frae Marie's heart!
　　But the thing it wou'dna be.

Oh, she has row'd it in her apron,
　　And set it on the sea:
"Gae sink ye, or swim ye, bonnie babe,
　　Ye'se get nae mair of me."

Word is to the kitchen gane,
    And word is to the ha',
And word is to the noble room,
    Amang the ladyes a',
That Marie Hamilton's brought to bed,
    And the bonnie babe's miss'd and awa.

Scarcely had she lain down again,
    And scarcely fa'en asleep,
When up then started our good Queen,
    Just at her bed-feet;

Saying — "Marie Hamilton, where's your babe?
    For I'm sure I heard it greet."

"Oh no, oh no, my noble Queen!
    Think no such thing to be;
'Twas but a stitch into my side,
    And sair it troubles me."

"Get up, get up, Marie Hamilton:
    Get up and follow me;
For I am going to Edinburgh town,
    A rich wedding to see."

Oh, slowly, slowly raise she up,
    And slowly put she on;
And slowly rode she out the way,
    With mony a weary groan.

The Queen was clad in scarlet,
    Her merry maids all in green;
And every town that they came to,
    They took Marie for the Queen.

"Ride hooly, hooly, gentlemen,
    Ride hooly now with me!
For never, I am sure, a wearier burd
    Rade in your companie."

But little wist Marie Hamilton,
    When she rade on the brown,
That she was gaen to Edinburgh town,
    And all to be put down.

"Why weep ye so, ye burgess wives,
    Why look ye so on me?
Oh, I am going to Edinburgh town,
    A rich wedding to see."

When she gaed up the tolbooth stairs,
    The corks frae her heels did flee;
And lang or e'er she came down again,
    She was condemn'd to dee.

When she came to the Netherbow Port,
    She laugh'd loud laughters three;
But when she came to the gallows foot,
    The tears blinded her e'e.

"Oh, happy, happy is the maid
    That's born of beauty free!
It was my dimpling rosie cheeks
    That's been the dule of me.

"Yestreen the Queen had four Maries,
    The night she'll ha'e but three;
There was Marie Seaton, and Marie Beaton,
    And Marie Carmichael, and me.

"Oh, often have I dress'd my Queen,
    And put gold upon her hair;
But now I've gotten, for my reward,
    The gallows to be my share.

"Oh, often have I dress'd my Queen,
    And often made her bed;
But now I've gotten, for my reward,
    The gallows tree to tread.

"I charge ye all, ye mariners,
    When ye sail o'er the faem,
Let neither my father nor mother get wit,
    But that I'm coming hame.

"I charge ye all, ye mariners,
    That sail upon the sea,
Let neither my father nor mother get wit,
    This dog's death I'm to dee.

"For if my father and mother got wit,
    And my bold brethren three,
Oh, meikle wou'd be the gude red bluid
    This day wou'd be spilt for me!

"Oh, little did my mother ken,
    That day she cradled me,
The lands I was to travel in,
    Or the death I was to dee!"

# ■ Sonnet

First *Ioue*, as greatest God aboue the rest,
Graunt thou to me a pairt of my desyre:
That when in verse of thee I wryte my best,
This onely thing I earnestly requyre,
That thou my veine Poetique so inspyre,
As they may suirlie think, all that it reid,
When I descryue thy might and thundring fyre,

That they do see thy self in verie deid
From heauen thy greatest *Thunders* for to leid,
And syne vpon the *Gyants* heads to fall:
Or cumming to thy *Semele* with speid
In *Thunders* least, at her request and call:
    Or throwing *Phaethon* downe from heauen to eard,
    With threatning thunders, making monstrous reard.

James VI (1566-1625)

# To Queen Anne
# on a New Year's Day 1604

Who knows your greatness, cannot but with fear
Draw near your altar, to make offrings there;
But whoso knows your goodness, may make bold,
And with a mite as with a mine of gold,
As confidently sacrifice to you:
And this is it that must plead pardon now,
Both for the poorness of my gifts and lines.
Princes are Gods, Gods laugh to see their shrines
Adorn'd with any gift but of that kind,
That beggars may as well as Croesus find:
They know how worldlings personate their parts,
And mask with gold presents of leaden hearts.
They know how gifts at Court are but a train
To steal from great ones twice as good again.
Now I have no such end; my poor oblation
At this auspicious time of salutation,
Had it a tongue, this only would it say,
Heav'ns heap upon you many a New-Year's Day.

Sir Robert Ayton (1570-1638)

# *From* An Exhortation to Prince Henry

I, Henry, hope with this mine eyes to feed,
   Whilst, ere thou wear'st a crown, thou wear'st a shield,
And when thou, making thousands once to bleed
   That dare behold thy count'nance and not yield,
Stirr'st through the bloody dust a foaming steed.
   An interested witness in the field,
I may amongst those bands thy grace attend,
And be thy Homer when the wars do end.

But stay, where fliest thou, Muse, so far astray?
   And whilst affection doth thy course command,
Dar'st thus above thy reach attempt a way
   To court the heir of Albion's warlike land,
Who gotten hath, his generous thoughts to sway,
   A royal gift out of a royal hand,
And hath before his eyes that type of worth,
That star of state, that pole which guides the north.

Yet o'er thy father, lo, such is thy fate,
   Thou hast this vantage which may profit thee —
An orphaned infant, settled in his seat,
   He greater than himself could never see,
Where thou may'st learn by him the art of state,
   And by another what thyself should'st be,
Whilst that which he had only but heard told,
In all his course thou practised may'st behold,

And this advantage long may'st thou retain,
   By which to make thee blest the heavens conspire,
And labour of his worth to make thy gain,
   To whose perfections thou may'st once aspire;
When as thou shew'st thyself, whilst thou dost reign,
   A son held worthy of so great a sire,
And with his sceptres and the people's hearts,
Dost still inherit his heroic parts.

Sir William Alexander (c1567-1640)

# On the Prince's Death, to the King

Did you ever see the day
When Blossomes fell in middst of May?
Rather, did you ever see
all ye Blossomes on the Tree
grow to ripe fruit? some must fall,
Nature sayes so, though not all.
    Though one be fallen, we have store,
    the Tree is fresh, & may have more.

And for our comfort this we know,
the soyle is good, and you may sowe.
What would we more? more seed cast on,
for so have thriving husbandes done.
And though ye first Cropp fayle, they find
a fruitfull earth will still be kind;
    And, sir, your patience is but Iust,
    for live we may but dye we must.

But this was ye first? tis true
God shouldbe first serv'd, then you.
He that made ye Sun to shine
said, the first fruit shalbe mine.
And thinke it not a heavy doome,
for he that gives all, may take some.
    Godes will is done, and yet to you
    he will ordeynes a Blessing too.

A man begettes a man, the king
did more, begatt a holy thing;
An Angell, that nere knew offence,
such priviledge hath Innocence.
The king then cannot make Complaynt
when ye kinges first borne is a Saint;
    Nay more, an Angell, heavenly blesst,
    so let our heavenly Angell rest.

Sir Robert Ayton (1570-1638)

# To Prince Charles

That which I first for Henries life did sound,
Shall spite of death, which did high hopes betray,
A speaking pledge, a living token stay,
Which with his name shall make my love renown'd;
His successor, thou may'st make use of this,
Which freely showes what Princes doe deserve;
It both him dead, and thee alive may serve,
Thy fames presage, a monument of his.
That Charles of France, admir'd so much for worth,
Religious, valiant, was call'd justly Great;
Thou hast his name, strive for his worth and state,
Great in great Britaine, to adorn the North:
   That all the world with wondring eyes may see,
   What was from Henry hop'd, perform'd by thee.

Sir William Alexander (c1567-1640)

# Lines on the Execution of King Charles I

Great, good, and just, could I but rate
My grief, and thy too rigid fate,
I'd weep the world in such a strain
As it should deluge once again.
But since thy loud-tongued blood demands supplies
More from Briareus' hands than Argus' eyes,
I'll sing thine obsequies with trumpet sounds,
And write thine epitaph in blood and wounds.

James Graham, Marquis of Montrose (1612-1650)

# Nature, Birds, Animals

*From the 16th century right up to writers of today like Norman MacCaig, Derick Thomson and George MacBeth, Scotland has had excellent poets who have written about nature. The Cherrie and the Slae, by one of James VI's leading court poets, is a late flowering of the medieval tradition of "Roman de la Rose" and has many parallels in European literature, from Guillaume de Lorris and Jean de Meung to Chaucer himself. In that tradition, too, had been The Kingis Quair. When one gazes at the awesome vastness of Scotland's landscape — wild tracks of mountain, harsh rocks, lochs and moorlands so dear to the imagination of the Romantics, English as well as Scottish —, one might expect her poets to have represented nature with strong but undetailed descriptive energy. Yet the poetic eye, essentially, sees right into the heart of things, and records with loving detail the minutiae of a subject, so that its reality is conveyed to the reader with freshness and new insight. So we find Alexander Hume describing the busy, humming bees as "clogged", and James Thomson referring to a duck who "before her train rows garrulous". The crest of William Drummond's pet sparrow can be seen to "shake up and down" when the bird has been irritated by human visitors. To Fergusson, a gowd-spink (goldfinch) in captivity will "keek around at warblers free".*

*Poets take note not just of minutiae, but of minute creatures, too: like Fergusson's butterfly — "Daft gowk in macaroni dress" — and Ramsay's joke chameleon. Burns is, of course, Scotland's greatest nature poet. His To a Mountain Daisy and To a Mouse are justly famous for their simple sincerity, coupled with a deep insight into the essential relationship of man to the kingdom of nature. After Burns' mouse, read the homely, contemporary adaptation by the Dunfermline schoolmaster, Robert Henryson, of Aesop's fable about the town and country mice. This is a long poem, but not as difficult as it may look at first sight, and it repays any effort in reading it. Apart from its marvellous flavour of medieval town life in Scotland, it gives one of the most sympathetic and humorous insights into the "being" of animals in the whole pre-Romantic period.*

*There is complete contrast, too, between the sentiments of the Gaelic clipping blessing and those of the old gamekeeper, Duncan Ban MacIntyre, lamenting over the desolation of his haunts by the introduction of sheep-farms in the wake of the Highland Clearances.*

# *From* The Cherrie and the Slae

About ane bank, quhair birdis on bewis
Ten thusand tymis thair notis renewis
   Ilke houre into the day:
The Merle, & Maveis micht be sene,    *blackbird: thrush*
The Progne, and the Phelomene,    *swallow: nightingale*
   Quhilk caussit me to stay:
I lay and leynit me to ane bus,
   To heir the birdis beir,    *song*
Thair mirth was sa melodius,
   Throw nature of the yeir:
      Sum singing, sum springing,
        With wingis into the Sky:
      So trimlie, and nimlie,
        Thir birdis they flew me by.

I saw the Hurcheoun, and the Hair,    *hedgehog*
Quha fed amangis the flowris fair,
   Wer happing to and fro:
I saw the Cunning, and the Cat,    *rabbit*
Quhais downis with the dew was wat,
   With monie beistis mo:
The Hart, the Hynd, the Dae, the Rae,
   The Fowmart, and the Foxe    *pole-cat*
War skowping all fra brae to brae,
   Amang the wàter broxe.
      Sum feiding, sum dreiding,    *afraid*
        In cais of suddain snairis:
      With skipping, and tripping,
        They hantit all in pairis.

The air was sa attemperate,    *cool*
But ony myst Immaculate,    *without*
   Bot purefeit and cleir:
The flouris fair wer flurischit,
As nature had them nurischit,
   Baith delicate and deir:

And every blome on branche and bewch     *bough*
   So prettily wer spred,
And hang their heidis out ouir the hewch,     *crag*
   In Mayis colour cled.
     Sum knopping, sum dropping,     *budding*
      Of balmie liquor sweit:
     Distelling, and smelling,
      Throw Phoebus hailsum heit.

The Cukkow and the Cuschet cryde,     *wood-pigeon*
The Turtle on the uther syde,
   Na plesure had to play:
So schil in sorrow was her sang,     *shrill*
That throw her voce the roches rang,
   For Eccho answerit ay:
Lamenting sair *Narcissus* cace,
   Quha starvit at the well:
Quha with the shaddow of his face,
   For lufe did slay him sell:     *himself*
     Quhylis weiping, and creiping,
      About the well he baid:     *stayed*
     Quhylis lying, quhylis crying,
      Bot it na answere maid.

The dew as diamondis did hing,
Upon the tender twistis, and ying,     *twigs*
   Ouir-twinkling all the treis:
And ay quhair flowris flourischit faire,
Thair suddainly I saw repaire,
   In swarmes, the sownding beis:
Sum sweitly hes the hony socht,
   Quhil they war cloggit soir:     *burdened*
Sum willingly the waxe hes wrocht,
   To heip it up in stoir:
     So heiping, with keiping,
      Into thair hyvis they hyde it:
     Precyselie, and wyselie,
      For winter they provyde it.

To pen the pleasures of that Park,
How every blossome, branche, and bark,
   Agaynst the Sun did schyne:
I leif to Poetis to compyle,
In staitlie verse, and lofty style,
   It passis my ingyne:
Bot as I muffit myne allane,       *moved: alone*
   I saw an River rin
Outouir ane craggie Rok of stane,
   Syne lichtit in ane lin:      *lighted: pool*
      With tumbling, and rumbling,
        Amang the Rochis round:
      Dewalling, and falling.     *descending*
        Into that pit profound.

Alexander Montgomerie (c1545–c1610)

## *From* Of a Summer's Day

The golden globe incontinent,
Sets vp his shining head,
And ou'r the earth and firmament,
Displayes his beims abread.

   For ioy the birds with boulden throts,   *swollen*
Agains his visage shein,
Takes vp their kindelie musicke nots,   *natural*
In woods and gardens grein.

   Up braids the carefull husbandman,   *hastens*
His cornes, and vines to see,
And eurie tymous artisan,   *early rising*
In buith worke busilie.   *booth*

The pastor quits the slouthfull sleepe,        *herdsmen*
And passis forth with speede,
His little camow-nosed sheepe,                  *crooked*
And rowtting kie to feede.                      *lowing*

The passenger from perrels sure,               *perils*
Gangs gladly foorth the way:
Breife, everie liuing creature,
Takes comfort of the day,

The subtile mottie rayons light,               *rays of motes*
At rifts thay are in wonne,                     *have entered*
The glansing thains, and vitre bright,          *vanes: glass*
Resplends against the sunne.

The dew vpon the tender crops,
Lyke pearles white and round,
Or like to melted silver drops,
Refreshes all the ground.

The mystie rocke, the clouds of raine,          *vapour*
From tops of mountaines skails,                 *melts*
Cleare are the highest hils and plaine,
The vapors takes the vails.

Begaried is the saphire pend,                   *variegated: arch of the sky*
With spraings of skarlet hew,
And preciously from end till end,
Damasked white and blew.

The ample heauen of fabrik sure,
In cleannes dois surpas,
The chrystall and the siluer pure,
Or clearest poleist glas.

The time sa tranquill is and still,
That na where sall ye find,
Saife on ane high, and barren hill,
Ane aire of peeping wind.                       *whispering*

All trees and simples great and small,      *herbs*
That balmie leife do beir,
Nor thay were painted on a wall,
Na mair they moue or steir.

Calme is the deepe, and purpour se,
Yee smuther nor the sand,                    *smoother*
The wals that woltring wont to be,           *waves: surging*
Are stable like the land.

Sa silent is the cessile air,                *yielding*
That euery cry and call,
The hils, and dails, and forrest fair,
Againe repeates them all.

The riuers fresh, the callor streames,       *cool*
Ou'r rockes can softlie rin,
The water cleare like chrystall seames,
And makes a pleasant din.

The fields, and earthly superfice,           *surface*
With verdure greene is spread,
And naturallie but artifice,                 *without*
In partie coulors cled.

The flourishes and fragrant flowres,         *blossom*
Throw Phœbus fostring heit,
Refresht with dew and siluer showres,
Casts vp ane odor sweit.

The clogged busie humming beis,              *burdened*
That neuer thinks to drowne,
On flowers and flourishes of treis,
Collects their liquor browne.

Alexander Hume (c1556-1609)

# *From* The Seasons

Should I my steps turn to the rural seat
Whose lofty elms and venerable oaks
Invite the rook, who high amid the boughs
In early Spring his airy city builds,
And ceaseless caws amusive; there, well-pleased,
I might the various polity survey
Of the mixed household-kind. The careful hen
Calls all her chirping family around,
Fed and defended by the fearless cock,
Whose breast with ardour flames, as on he walks
Graceful, and crows defiance. In the pond
The finely-checkered duck before her train
Rows garrulous. The stately-sailing swan
Gives out his snowy plumage to the gale,
And, arching proud his neck, with oary feet
Bears forward fierce, and guards his osier-isle,
Protective of his young. The turkey nigh,
Loud-threatening, reddens; while the peacock spreads
His every-coloured glory to the sun,
And swims in radiant majesty along.
O'er the whole homely scene the cooing dove
Flies thick in amorous chase, and wanton rolls
The glancing eye, and turns the changeful neck.
  While thus the gentle tenants of the shade
Indulge their purer loves, the rougher world
Of brutes below rush furious into flame
And fierce desire. Through all his lusty veins
The bull, deep-scorched, the raging passion feels.
Of pasture sick, and negligent of food,
Scarce seen he wades among the yellow broom,
While o'er his ample sides the rambling sprays
Luxuriant shoot; or through the mazy wood
Dejected wanders, nor the enticing bud
Crops, though it presses on his careless sense.
And oft, in jealous maddening fancy wrapt,
He seeks the fight; and, idly-butting, feigns
His rival gored in every knotty trunk.

Him should he meet, the bellowing war begins:
Their eyes flash fury; to the hollowed earth,
Whence the sand flies, they mutter bloody deeds,
And, groaning deep, the impetuous battle mix:
While the fair heifer, balmy-breathing near,
Stands kindling up their rage. The trembling steed,
With this hot impulse seized in every nerve,
Nor heeds the rein, nor hears the sounding thong;
Blows are not felt; but, tossing high his head,
And by the well-known joy to distant plains
Attracted strong, all wild he bursts away;
O'er rocks, and woods, and craggy mountains flies;
And, neighing, on the aerial summit takes
The exciting gale; then, steep-descending, cleaves
The headlong torrents foaming down the hills,
Even where the madness of the straitened stream
Turns in  black eddies round: such is the force
With which his frantic heart and sinews swell.

James Thomson (1700-1748)

## On Seeing a Butterfly in the Street

Daft gowk, in macaroni dress,
Are ye come here to shaw your face,
Bowden wi' pride o' simmer gloss,
To cast a dash at Reikie's cross;
And glowr at mony a twa-legg'd creature,
Flees, braw by art, tho' worms by nature?

Like country laird in city cleeding,
Ye're come to town to lear' good breeding;
To bring ilk darling toast and fashion
In vogue amang the flee creation,
That they, like buskit belles and beaux,

69

May crook their mou' fu' sour at those
Whase weird is still to creep, alas!
Unnotic'd 'mang the humble grass;
While you, wi' wings new buskit trim,
Can far frae yird and reptiles skim;
Newfangle grown wi' new-got form,
You soar aboon your mither worm.

Kind Nature lent but for a day
Her wings to mak ye sprush and gay;
In her habuliments a while
Ye may your former sell beguile,
And ding awa' the vexing thought
O' hourly dwinin' into nought,
By beengin' to your foppish brithers,
Black corbies dress'd in peacock's feathers;
Like thee they dander here and there,
Whan Simmer's blinks are warm and fair,
And lo'e to snuff the healthy balm,
Whan E'enin' spreads her wing sae calm;
But whan she girns and glow'rs sae dour
Frae Borean houff in angry show'r,
Like thee they scour frae street or field,
And hap them in a lyther bield;
For they were never made to dree
The adverse gloom o' Fortune's e'e,
Nor ever pried life's pinin' woes,
Nor pu'd the prickles wi' the rose.

Poor Butterfly! thy case I mourn,
To green kail-yard and fruits return:
How could you troke the mavis' note
For "penny pies all-pipin' hot?"
Can lintie's music be compar'd
Wi' gruntles frae the City Guard?
Or can our flow'rs, at ten hour's bell,
The gowan or the spink excel?

Now shou'd our sclates wi' hailstanes ring,
What cabbage-fauld wad screen your wing;

Say, fluttering fairy! wert thy hap
To light beneath braw Nanny's cap,
Wad she, proud butterfly of May!
In pity let you skaithless gae?
The furies glancing frae her een
Wad rug your wings o' siller sheen,
That, wae for thee! far, far outvy
Her Paris artist's finest dye;
Then a your bonny spraings wad fall,
And you a worm be left to crawl.

To sic mishanter rins the laird
Wha quits his ha'-house and kail-yard,
Grows politician, scours to court,
Whare he's the laughing-stock and sport
O' Ministers, wha jeer and jibe,
And heeze his hopes wi' thought o' bribe,
Till in the end they flae him bare,
Leave him to poortith, and to care.
Their fleetchin' words owre late he sees,
He trudges hame, repines, and dies.

Sic be their fa' wha dirk their ben
In blackest business nae their ain;
And may they scad their lips fu' leal,
That dip their spoons in ither's kail.

Robert Fergusson (1750-1774)

# To a Mouse
## On turning her up in her nest, with the plough, November 1785

Wee, sleekit, cowrin, tim'rous beastie,
O, what a panic's in thy breastie!
Thou need na start awa sae hasty,
   Wi' bickering brattle!
I wad be laith to rin an' chase thee,
   Wi' murd'ring pattle!

I'm truly sorry Man's dominion
Has broken Nature's social union,
An' justifies that ill opinion,
   Which makes thee startle,
At me, thy poor, earth-born companion,
   An' fellow-mortal!

I doubt na, whyles, but thou may thieve;
What then? poor beastie, thou maun live!
A daimen icker in a thrave
   'S a sma' request:
I'll get a blessin wi' the lave,
   And never miss't!

Thy wee bit housie, too, in ruin!
Its silly wa's the win's are strewin!
An' naething, now, to big a new ane,
   O' foggage green!
An' bleak December's winds ensuin,
   Baith snell and keen!

Thou saw the fields laid bare an' waste,
An' weary Winter comin fast,
An' cozie here, beneath the blast,
   Thou thought to dwell,
Till crash! the cruel coulter past
   Out thro' thy cell.

That wee bit heap o' leaves an' stibble,
Has cost thee mony a weary nibble!
Now thou's turn'd out, for a' thy trouble,
    But house or hald,
To thole the Winter's sleety dribble,
    An' cranreuch cauld!

But Mousie, thou art no thy lane,
In proving foresight may be vain:
The best-laid schemes o' Mice an' Men
    Gang aft a-gley,
An' lea'e us nought but grief and pain,
    For promis'd joy.

Still thou art blest, compar'd wi' me!
The present only toucheth thee:
But, Och! I backward cast my e'e,
    On prospects drear!
An' forward, tho' I canna see,
    I guess an' fear!

Robert Burns (1759-1796)

# The Tale of the Country Mouse and the Town Mouse

Esope myne authour makis mentioun
Of twa myis, and thay wer sisteris deir,
Of quham the eldest duelt in ane borous-toun,
The uther wynnit uponland weill neir,                    *lived*
Soliter, quhyle under busk, quhyle under breir,
Quhilis in the corne, and uther mennis skaith,          *harm*
As owtlawis dois and levis on thair waith.              *hunting*


This rurall mous into the wynter-tyde
Had hunger, cauld, and tholit grit distres;
The uther mous that in the burgh can byde,
Was gild-brother and made ane fre burges —
Toll-fre als, but custum mair or les,
And fredome had to ga quhairever scho list,
Amang the cheis in ark, and meill in kist.             *box*


Ane tyme quhen scho wes full and unfutesair,
Scho tuke in mynd hir sister uponland,
And langit for to heir of hir weilfair,
To se quhat lyfe scho had under the wand:               *in the country*
Bairfute, allone, with pykestaf in hir hand,
As pure pylgryme scho passit owt off town,
To seik hir sister baith oure daill and down.


Furth mony wilsum wayis can scho walk;
Throw mosse and mure, throw bankis, busk and breir,
Scho ran cryand quhill scho come to a balk:             *untilled piece of ground*
"Cum furth to me, my awin sister deir;
Cry peip anis!" With that the mous culd heir,           *squeak: once*
And knew hir voce, as kinnisman will do,
Be verray kynd; and furth scho come hir to.

The hartlie joy God geve ye had sene
Beis kith quhen that thir sisteris met!                    *shown*
And grit kyndnes wes schawin thame betuene,
For quhylis thay leuch, and quhylis for joy thay gret,
Quhyle kissit sweit, quhylis in armis plet;               *embrace*
And thus thay fure quhill soberit wes thair mude,
Syne fute for fute unto the chalmer yude.                 *then: chamber*

As I hard say, it was ane sober wane,                     *home*
Off fog and farne full febilie wes maid —                 *moss: fern*
Ane sillie scheill under ane steidfast stane,             *poor: dwelling-place*
Off quhilk the entres wes not hie nor braid;
And in the samin thay went but mair abaid,                *delay*
Without fyre or candill birnand bricht,
For comonly sic pykeris luffis not lycht.                 *pilferers*

Quhen thay wer lugit thus, thir sely myse,
The youngest sister into hir butterie glyde,
And brocht furth nuttis and candill insteid off spyce;
Giff this wes gude fair, I do it on thame besyde.         *leave them to say*
The burges-mous prompit forth in pryde,
And said: "Sister, is this your dayly fude?"
"Quhy not?" quod scho. "Is not this meit rycht gude?"

"Na, be my saull, I think it bot ane scorne."
"Madame," quod scho, "ye be the mair to blame;
My mother sayd, sister, quhen we wer borne,
That I and ye lay baith within ane wame:
I keip the rate and custome off my dame,
And off my leving into povertie,
For landis have we nane in propertie."

"My fair sister," quod scho, "have me excusit —
This rude dyat and I can not accord;
To tender meit my stomok is ay usit,
For quhylis I fair als weill as ony lord;
Thir wydderit peis and nuttis, or thay be bord,          *stale: pierced*
Wil brek my teith, and mak my wame ful sklender,         *stomach*
Quhilk wes before usit to meitis tender."

75

"Weil, weil, sister," quod the rurall mous,
"Geve it pleis yow, sic thing as ye se heir,
Baith meit and dreink, harberie and hous,                    *lodging*
Sal be your awin, will ye remane al yeir;
Ye sall it have wyth blyith and mery cheir —
And that suld mak the maissis that ar rude,                  *dishes: simple*
Amang freindis, richt tender and wonder gude.

"Quhat plesure is in the feistis delicate,
The quhilkis ar gevin with ane glowmand brow?               *frowning*
Ane gentill hart is better recreate
With blyith curage, that seith to him ane kow;              *if an ox were cooked*
Ane modicum is mair for till allow,
Swa that gude will be kerver at the dais,
Than thrawin vult and mony spycit mais."                    *sour countenance: dishes*

For all hir mery exhortatioun,
This burges-mous had littill will to sing;
Bot hevilie scho kest hir browis doun
For all the daynteis that scho culd hir bring.
Yit at the last scho said, halff in hething:                *mockery*
"Sister, this victuall and your royall feist
May weill suffice unto ane rurall beist.

"Lat be this hole, and cum into my place;
I sall to yow schaw be experience
My Gude Friday is better nor your Pace;
My dische-likingis is worth your haill expence.
I have housis anew off grit defence;                        *enough*
Off cat nor fall-trap I have na dreid."
"I grant," quod scho; and on togidder thay yeid.            *went*

In stubbill array throw gers and corne,                     *with difficulty*
And under buskis prevelie couth thay creip —                *privately*
The eldest wes the gyde and went beforne,
The younger to hir wayis tuke gude keip;                    *heed*
On nicht thay ran, and on the day can sleip,
Quhill in the morning, or the laverok sang,
Thay fand the town, and in blythlie couth gang.

76

ot fer fra thyne unto ane worthie wane,                          *dwelling*
his burges brocht thame sone quhare thay suld be;
ithowt "God speid!" thair harberie wes tane,                     *straightway*
to ane spence with vittell grit plentie;                         *larder*
ith cheis and butter upon thair skelfis hie,
d flesche and fische aneuch, baith fresche and salt,
d sekkis full off meill and eik off malt.

ir quhen thay disposit wer to dyne,
ithowtin grace thay wesche and went to meit,
ith all coursis that cukis culd devyne —
uttoun and beif, strikin in tailyeis greit;                      *cut: portions*
e lordis fair thus couth thay counterfeit —
cept ane thing — thay drank the watter cleir
steid off wyne: bot yit thay maid gude cheir.

ith blyith upcast and merie countenance,
e eldest sister sperit at hir gest                               *asked*
ff that scho be ressone fand difference                         *with good reason*
tuix that chalmer and hir sarie nest.                            *poor*
e, dame," quod scho, "how lang will this lest?"
or evermair, I wait, and langer to."
iff it be swa, ye ar at eis," quod scho.

l eik thair cheir ane subcharge furth scho brocht —             *extra course*
e plait off grottis, and ane dische full off meill;             *groats*
raf-caikkis als I trow scho spairit nocht                       *oat-cakes*
oundantlie about hir for to deill;
d mane full fyne scho brocht insteid off geill,                 *white bread: jelly*
d ane quhyte candill owt off ane coffer stall,                  *box: stolen*
teid off spyce to gust thair mouth withall.                     *give them relish*

is maid thay merie quhill thay micht na mair,
d "Haill, Yule! Haill!" cryit upon hie.
efter joy oftymes cummis cair,
d troubill efter grit prosperitie:
us as thay sat in all thair jolitie,
e spenser come with keyis in his hand,                          *steward*
pinnit the dure, and thame at denner fand.

Thay taryit not to wesche, as I suppose,
Bot on to ga quha that micht formest win.
The burges had ane hole, and in scho gois;
Hir sister had na hole to hyde hir in:
To se that selie mous it wes grit sin,
So desolate and will off ane gude reid;                    *at her wits' end*
For verray dreid scho fell in swoun neir deid.

Bot as God wald, it fell ane happie cace;
The spenser had na laser for to byde,                      *leisure*
Nowther to seik nor serche, to sker nor chace;
But on he went, and left the dure up wyde.
The bald burges his passing weill hes spyde;
Out off hir hole scho come and cryit on hie:
"How fair ye sister? Cry peip quhairever ye be!"

This rurall mous lay flatling on the ground,
And for the deith scho wes full sair dredand,
For till hir hart straik mony wofull stound;
As in ane fever scho trimbillit fute and hand.
And quhan hir sister in sic ply hir fand,
For verray pietie scho began to greit,
Syne confort hir with wordis hunny-sweit.

"Quhy ly ye thus? Ryse up, my sister deir!
Cum to your meit; this perrell is overpast."
The uther answerit hir with hevie cheir:
"I may not eit, sa sair I am agast!
I had lever thir fourty dayis fast,
With watter-caill, and to gnaw benis or peis,             *meatless broth*
Than all your feist in this dreid and diseis."            *discomfort*

With fair tretie yit scho gart hir upryse,
And to the burde thay went and togidder sat;              *table*
And scantlie had thay drunkin anis or twyse,
Quhen in come Gib Hunter, our jolie cat,
And bad "God speid!" The burges up with that
And till hir hole scho went as fyre on flint;
Bawdronis the uther be the bak hes hint.                  *Puss: seized*

Fra fute to fute he kest hir to and fra,
Quhylis up, quhylis doun, als cant as ony kid; *merry*
Quhylis wald he lat hir rin under the stra,
Quhylis wald he wink, and play with hir buk-heid. *blind-man's buff*
Thus to the selie mous grit pane he did,
Quhill at the last, throw fortune and gude hap,
Betwix ane burde and the wall scho crap. *wainscoating*

And up in haist behind ane parraling *partition*
scho clam so hie that Gilbert micht not get hir —
Syne be the cluke thair craftelie can hing *claws*
Till he wes gane; hir cheir wes all the better;
Syne doun scho lap quhen thair wes nane to let hir, *prevent*
And to the burges-mous loud can scho cry:
Fairweill, sister, thy feist heir I defy! *reject*

Thy mangerie is mingit all with cair —
Thy guse is gude, thy gansell sour as gall; *sauce*
The subcharge off thy service is bot sair —
Sa sall thow find heir efterwart na fall.
I thank yone courtyne and yone perpall wall *curtain: partition*
Off my defence now fra yone crewell beist.
Almichtie God keip me fra sic ane feist!

Wer I into the kith that I come fra, *place*
For weill nor wo suld I never cum agane."
With that scho tuke hir leif and furth can ga,
Quhylis throw the corne, and quhylis throw the plane:
Quhen scho wes furth and fre, scho wes full fane, *glad*
And merilie markit unto the mure. *went: moor*
I can not tell how weill thairefter scho fure.

Bot I hard say scho passit to hir den,
Als warme as woll, suppose it wes not greit,
Full beinly stuffit, baith but and ben,
Off beinis, and nuttis, peis, ry and quheit;
Quhenever scho list, scho had aneuch to eit,
In quyet and eis, withoutin ony dreid;
Bot to hir sisteris feist na mair scho yeid. *went*

## Moral

Freindis, ye may find, and ye will tak heid,
Into this fabill ane gude moralitie:
As fitchis myngit ar with nobill seid,                    *vetches*
Swa interminglit is adversitie
With eirdlie joy, swa that na estate is frie,
Without trubill and sum vexatioun —
And namelie thay quhilk clymmis up maist hie,
That ar not content with small possessioun.

Blissed be sempill lyfe withoutin dreid;
Blissed be sober feist in quietie:
Quha hes aneuch, of na mair hes he neid,
Thocht it be littill into quantatie.
Grit aboundance and blind prosperitie
Oftymes makis ane evill conclusioun;
The sweitest lyfe, thairfoir, in this cuntrie,
Is sickernes with small possessioun.                      *security*

O wantoun man, that usis for to feid
Thy wambe, and makis it a god to be,
Luke to thy self! I warne the weill; but dreid            *assuredly*
The cat cummis, and to the mous hes ee.
Quhat vaillis than thy feist and royaltie
With dreidfull hart and tribulatioun?
Best thing in eird, thairfoir, I say for me,
Is blyithnes in hart, with small possessioun.

Thy awin fyre, my freind, sa it be bot ane gleid,         *ember*
It warmis weill, and is worth gold to the;
And Solomon sayis, gif that thow will reid:
"Under the hevin thair can not better be
Than ay be blyith and leif in honestie."                  *live*
Quhairfoir I may conclude be this ressoun:                *declaration*
Of eirthly joy it beiris maist degre,
Blyithnes in hart, with small possessioun.

Robert Henryson (fl.c1480-c1490)

# The Chamaeleon

Twa Travellers, as they were wa'king,
'Bout the *Chamaeleon* fell a ta'king,
(Sic think it shaws them mettl'd Men,
To say I've seen, and ought to ken;)
Says ane, 'Tis a strange Beast indeed,
Four-footed, with a Fish's Head;
A little Bowk, with a lang Tail,
And moves far slawer than a Snail;
Of Colour like a Blawart blue; —
Reply'd his Nibour, *That's no true;*
*For well I wat his Colour's Green,*
*If ane may true his ain twa Een;*
*For I in Sun-shine saw him fair,*
*When he was dining on the Air.* —
Excuse me, says the ither Blade,
I saw him better in the Shade,
And he is Blue. — *He's Green I'm sure.* —
Ye lied. — *And ye're the Son of a Whore.* —
Frae Words there had been Cuff and Kick,
Had not a Third come in the Nick,
Wha tenting them in this rough Mood,
Cry'd, Gentlemen, what! are ye wood?
What's ye'r Quarrel, and't may be speer't?
Truth, says the tane, Sir, ye shall hear't:
The *Chamaeleon,* I say, he's Blue;
He threaps he's Green. — Now, what say you?
Ne'er fash ye'r sells about the Matter,
Says the sagacious Arbitrator,
He's Black. — Sae nane of you are right,
I view'd him well with Candle-light;
And have it in my Pocket here,
Row'd in my Napkin hale and feer.
*Fy!* said ae Cangler, *What d'ye mean?*
*I'll lay my Lugs on't, that he's Green.*
Said th'ither, were I gawn to Death,
I'd swear he's Blue with my last Breath.
He's Black, the Judge maintain'd ay stout;

And to convince them, whop'd him out:
But to Surprise of ane and a',
The *Animal* was White as Snaw,
And thus reprov'd them, "Shallow Boys,
   "Away, away, make nae mair Noise;
   Ye're a' three wrang, and a' three right,
   But learn to own your Nibours Sight
   As good as yours. — Your Judgment speak,
   But never be sae daftly weak
   T'imagine ithers will by Force
   Submit their Sentiments to yours;
   As things in various Lights ye see,
   They'll ilka ane resemble me."

Allan Ramsay (1684-1758)

# The Clipping Blessing

Go shorn and come woolly,
Bear the Beltane female lamb,
Be the lovely Bride thee endowing,
And the fair Mary thee sustaining,
   The fair Mary sustaining thee.

Michael the chief be shielding thee
From the evil dog and from the fox,
From the wolf and from the sly bear,
And from the taloned birds of destructive bills,
   From the taloned birds of hooked bills.

Translated from the Gaelic<br>by Alexander Carmichael

82

# A Song of Foxes

Ho! ho! ho! the foxes!
Would there were more of them,
I'd give heavy gold
For a hundred score of them!

My blessing with the foxes dwell,
For that they hunt the sheep so well!

Ill fa' the sheep, a grey-faced nation,
That swept our hills with desolation!

Who made the bonnie green glens clear,
And acres scarce, and houses dear;

The grey-faced sheep, who worked our woe,
Where men no more may reap or sow,

And made us leave for their grey pens
Our bonnie braes and grassy glens,

Where we were reared, and gladly grew,
And lived to kin and country true;

Who bared the houses to the wind,
Where hearths were warm, and hearts were kind,

And spread the braes with wreck and ruin,
The grey-faced sheep for our undoing!

And where they came were seen no more
Harrow or hoe on slope or shore,

And on the old and friendly places
New people sit with loveless faces;

And the good grey mare no more is seen
With its frisking foal on the open green,

And I seek in vain for the cow that lay
Licking its calf on the bonnie green brae!

And the bonnie milk-maids, ohon! ohon!
Are seen no more when the kine are gone!

And there's now no work for the lads to do
But to herd the sheep — some one or two!

And the goats, whose mild was good and cheap,
They too must go, to make way for the sheep!

And the roe in the rocky glade that lies
Is waked no more by the fawn when it cries.

For stags will flee, and mothers will weep,
When gentlemen live to make money by sheep!

And foresters now can earn no penny
Where stags are few and sheep are many.

He earns from me no kindly will
Who harms the fox upon the hill;

May he die the death of a hog
Against a fox who drives a dog!

On the hill-side may he rot
Who fires on Reynard with cruel shot!

And may the young cubs prosper well
Where snug in rocky holes they dwell!

And if my prayer with Heaven prevail
No trap shall grip their bushy tail!

And may they live on tasteful food,
And die as wise old foxes should!

Duncan Ban MacIntyre (1724-1812)
Translated from the Gaelic
by John Stuart Blackie

## Translation of the Death of a Sparrow, out of Passerat

Ah! if yee aske (my friendes) why this salt shower
My blubbered eyes vpon this paper power,
Dead is my sparrow; he whom I did traine,
And turnd so toward, by a cat is slaine.
Skipping no more now shall hee on me attend.
Light displeaseth: would my dayes could end!
Ill heare no more him chirpe forth prettye layes;
Haue I not cause to curse my wretched dayes?
A Dedalus hee was to snatch a flye,
Nor wrath nor wildnesse men in him could spye;
If to assault his taile that any dard,
He pinchd their fingers, and against them warrd:
Then might bee seene the crest shake vp & down,
Which fixed was vpon his litle crown;
Like Hectores, Troyes strong bulwarke, when in ire
Hee ragd to set the Grecian fleet on fire.
But ah, alas! a cat this pray espyes,
Then with a traitrous leap did it surprise.

Vndoubtedlie this bird was killd by treason,
Or otherwise should of that feind had reason.
So Achilles thus by Phrigian heard was slaine,
And stout Camilla fell by Aruns vaine:
So that false horse which Pallas raisd gainst Troy,
Priame & that faire cittye did destroy.
Thou now, whose heart is swelled with this vaine glorye,
Shalt not liue long to count thy honours storye.
If any knowledge bideth after death
In sprites of Birdes whose bodyes haue no breath,
My dearlings sprit sal know in lower place,
The vangeance falling on the cattish race.
For neuer chat nor catling I sal find,
But mawe they shall in Plutos palace blind.
Ye who with panted pens & bodies light
Doe dint the aire, turne hadervart your flight,
To my sad teares apply these notes of yours,
Vnto this Idol bring a Harvest of flours;
Let him accepte from vs, as most deuine,
Sabean incense, milke, food, suetest vine;
And on a stone these vords let some engraue:
The litle Body of a sparrow braue
In a foul gloutonous chats vombe closd remaines,
Vhose ghost now graceth the Elysian plaines.

William Drummond of Hawthornden (1585-1649)

# Ode to the Gowdspink

Frae fields where Spring her sweets has blawn
Wi' caller verdure owre the lawn,
The Gowdspink comes in new attire,
The brawest 'mang the whistling choir,
That, ere the sun can clear his een,
Wi' glib notes sane the Simmer's green.

Sure Nature herried mony a tree,
For spraings and bonny spats to thee:
Nae mair the rainbow can impart
Sic glowin ferlies o' her art,
Whase pencil wrought its freaks at will
On thee, the sey-piece o' her skill.
Nae mair thro' straths in Simmer dight
We seek the rose to bless our sight;
Or bid the bonny wa'-flowers sprout
On yonder ruin's lofty snout.
Thy shinin garments far outstrip
The cherries upo' Hebe's lip,
And fool the tints that Nature chose
To busk and paint the crimson rose.

'Mang men, wae's heart! we aften find
The brawest drest want peace o' mind,
While he that gangs wi' ragged coat
Is weel contentit wi' his lot.
Whan wand wi' glewy birdlime's set,
To steal far aff your dautit mate,
Blithe wad ye change your cleeding gay
In lieu of lav'rock's sober gray.
In vain thro' woods you sair may ban
The envious treachery of man,
That wi' your gowden glister ta'en,
Still hunts you on the Simmer's plain,
And traps you 'mang the sudden fa's
O' Winter's dreary, dreepin snaws.
Now steekit frae the gowany field,

Frae ilka fav'rite houff and beild;
But mergh, alas! to disengage
Your bonny buik frae fettering cage,
Your free-born bosom beats in vain
For darling liberty again.
In window hung, how aft we see
Thee keek around at warblers free,
That carol saft, and sweetly sing
Wi' a' the blitheness o' the Spring?
Like Tantalus they hing you here
To spy the glories o' the year;
And tho' you're at the burnie's brink,
They douna suffer you to drink.

Ah, Liberty! thou bonny dame,
How wildly wanton is thy stream
Round whilk the birdies a' rejoice,
And hail you wi' a gratefu' voice.
The Gowdspink chatters joyous here,
And courts wi' gleesome sangs his peer:
The mavis frae the new-bloom'd thorn
Begins his lauds at earest morn;
And herd lowns loupin o'er the grass,
Need far less fleetchin to their lass,
Than paughty damsels bred at courts,
Wha thraw their mou's, and tak the dorts;
But, reft of thee, fient flee we care
For a' that life ahint can spare.
The Gowdspink, that sae lang has kend
Thy happy sweets (his wonted friend),
Her sad confinement ill can brook
In some dark chaumer's dowie nook;
Tho' Mary's hand his nebb supplies,
Unkend to hunger's painfu' cries,
Ev'n beauty canna chear the heart
Frae life, frae liberty apart;
For now we tyne its wonted lay,
Sae lightsome, sweet, sae blithely gay.

Thus Fortune aft a curse can gie,
To wyle us far frae liberty;
Then tent her syren smiles wha list,
I'll ne'er envy your girnel's grist;
For whan fair Freedom smiles nae mair,
Care I for life? Shame fa' the hair;
A field o'ergrown wi' rankest stubble,
The essence o' a paltry bubble.

Robert Fergusson (1750-1774)

## To a Mountain Daisy
## On turning one down with the plough, in April 1786

Wee, modest, crimson-tipped flow'r,
Thou's met me in an evil hour;
For I maun crush amang the stour
    Thy slender stem:
To spare thee now is past my pow'r,
    Thou bonie gem.

Alas! it's no thy neibor sweet,
The bonie lark, companion meet,
Bending thee 'mang the dewy weet,
    Wi' spreckl'd breast!
When upward-springing, blythe, to greet
    The purpling east.

Cauld blew the bitter-biting north
Upon thy early, humble birth;
Yet cheerfully thou glinted forth
    Amid the storm,
Scarce rear'd above the parent-earth
    Thy tender form.

The flaunting flow'rs our gardens yield,
High shelt'ring woods and wa's maun shield;
But thou, beneath the random bield
    O' clod or stane,
Adorns the histie stibble field,
    Unseen, alane.

There, in the scanty mantle clad,
Thy snawie bosom sun-ward spread,
Thou lifts thy unassuming head
    In humble guise;
But now the share uptears thy bed,
    And low thou lies!

Such is the fate of artless maid,
Sweet flow'ret of the rural shade!
By love's simplicity betray'd,
    And guileless trust;
Till she, like thee, all soil'd, is laid
    Low i' the dust.

Such is the fate of simple bard,
On life's rough ocean luckless starr'd!
Unskilful he to note the card
    Of prudent lore,
Till billows rage, and gales blow hard,
    And whelm him o'er!

Such fate to suffering worth is giv'n,
Who long with wants and woes has striv'n,
By human pride or cunning driv'n
    To mis'ry's brink;
Till wrench'd of ev'ry stay but Heav'n,
    He, ruin'd, sink!

Ev'n thou who mourn'st the Daisy's fate,
That fate is thine — no distant date;
Stern Ruin's plough-share drives elate,
    Full on thy bloom,
Till crush'd beneath the furrow's weight,
    Shall be thy doom!

Robert Burns (1759-1796)

# The Sea

*For so many Scots, the sea has been their life. To those who are surrounded by water — and Scotland has a proportion of coastline to land area which is very high, to say nothing of her myriad islands, many of which have been at some time inhabited —, the sea is an object of respect, awe and fear. It is only to be expected, then, that shipwrecks are the subject of many poems and ballads, and that Scottish poets have shown great understanding of the sea and ships. Gavin Douglas's description of the storm from Book 1 of the original is even more graphic than Virgil's, and if Douglas did not know the sea himself, his cousin Henry Lord St Clair, who apparently suggested to the poet that he translate the Aeneid, certainly did: for he was captain of James IV's warship, "The Great Michael". William Falconer actually was, for most of his life, a professional seaman, and was finally drowned at sea. The juxta-position of Falconer's heroic style with his contemporary Fergusson's mock-heroics is deliberate. And, yes, gentle reader, the words of Rule Britannia were written by a Scot, though whether it was David Mallet (originally called Malloch) or James Thomson, who collaborated with Mallet to produce "The Masque of Alfred" in which it originally appeared in this form, is not clear. Alexander Macdonald lived almost all his life on the West Highland coast. His long poem The Birlinn of Clanranald (birlinn means a "galley") describes a sea journey from Uist to Ireland. Maybe, such a voyage was preceded by the Gaelic blessing with which this section ends.*

# Sir Patrick Spens

The king sits in Dunfermline town,
    Drinking the bluid-red wine:
"Oh, where will I get a gude skipper
    To sail this ship of mine?"

It's up and spake an eldern knight,
    Sat at the king's right knee —
"Sir Patrick Spens is the best sailor
    That ever sail'd the sea."

The king has written a braid letter,
    And seal'd it with his hand,
And sent it to Sir Patrick Spens,
    Was walking on the strand.

"To Noroway, to Noroway,
    To Noroway o'er the faem!
The king's daughter to Noroway,
    'Tis thou maun take her hame!"

The first line that Sir Patrick read,
    A loud, loud laugh laugh'd he;
But ere he read it to an end,
    The tear blinded his e'e.

"Oh, wha is this has done this deed,
    And tauld the king of me, —
To send us out at this time of the year,
    To sail upon the sea?

"Be't wind, be't weet, be't hail, be't sleet,
    Our ship must sail the faem;
The king's daughter to Noroway,
    'Tis we must take her hame."

They hoysed their sails on Monenday morn,
  With all the speed they may,
And they ha'e landed in Noroway
  Upon a Wodensday.

They hadna been a week, a week
  In Noroway, but twae,
When that the lords of Noroway
  Began aloud to say:

"Ye Scottishmen spend all our king's gowd,
  And all our young queen's fee."
"Ye lee, ye lee, ye liars loud!
  Full loud I hear ye lee!

"For I ha'e brought as much white monie
  As gane my men and me;
I brought a half-fou of guide red gowd
  Out o'er the sea with me.

"But betide me weil, betide me wae,
  This day I'se leave the shore;
And never spend my king's monie
  'Mong Noroway dogs no more."

Then out it spake a gude auld man,
  In Sir Patrick's companie:
"Whatever ye do, my gude master,
  Take God your guide to be."

"Make ready, make ready, my merry men all,
  Our gude ship sails the morn."
"Now, ever alake! my master dear,
  I fear a deadly storm!

"I saw the new moon, late yestreen,
  With the auld moon in her arm;
And if we gang to sea, master,
  I fear we'll come to harm."

Sir Patrick and his merry men all
    Were ance mair on the faem;
With five-and-fifty Scots lords' sons,
    That lang'd to be at hame.

But they hadna sail'd upon the sea
    A day but barely three,
When the lift grew dark, and the wind blew loud,
    And gurly grew the sea.

The ankers brak, and the topmasts lap,
    It was sic a deadly storm;
And the waves came o'er the broken ship
    Till all her sides were torn.

"Oh, where will I get a gude sailor
    To take my helm in hand,
Till I get up to the tall topmast,
    To see if I can spy land?"

"Oh, here am I, a sailor gude,
    To take the helm in hand,
Till you go up to the tall topmast;
    But I fear ye'll ne'er spy land."

Then up and came a mermaid wild,
    With a siller cup in her hand:
"Sail on, sail on, my gude Scots lords,
    For ye soon will see dry land."

"Awa, awa, ye mermaid wild,
    And let your fleechin' be;
For, since your face we've seen the day,
    Dry land we'll never see."

He hadna gane a step, a step,
    A step but barely ane,
When a bolt flew out of the goodly ship,
    And the saut sea it came in.

"Gae fetch a web of the silken claith,
    Another of the twine,
And wap them into our gude ship's side,
    And let na the sea come in."

They fetch'd a web of the silken claith,
    Another of the twine;
And they wapp'd them into the gude ship's side,
    But still the sea came in.

Oh, laith, laith were our gude Scots lords
    To weet their cork-heel'd shoon!
But lang or all the play was play'd,
    They wet their hats aboon.

And mony was the feather bed
    That floated on the faem;
And mony was the gude lord's son
    That never mair came hame.

Oh, lang, lang may the ladies sit,
    And gaze with fan in hand,
Before they see Sir Patrick Spens
    Come sailing to the strand.

And lang, lang may the maidens sit,
    With their gowd kaims in their hair,
A-waiting for their ain dear loves;
    For them they'll see nae mair.

Half ower, half ower to Aberdour,
    'Tis fifty fathoms deep;
And there lies gude Sir Patrick Spens,
    With the Scots lords at his feet.

# *From* The Aeneid

| | |
|---|---|
| Belive Eneas membris schuk for cald, | *at once* |
| And murnand baith his handis up did hald | *mourning* |
| Towart the sternys, with petuus voce thus gan say: | *stars* |
| "O sevin tymys quhou happy and blissit war thai | |
| Under hie wallis of Troy, by dynt of swerd, | *stroke* |
| Deit in thar faderis syght, bytand the erd! | *biting* |
| O thou of Grekis mast forcy, Diomed, | |
| Quhy mycht I not on feldis of Troy have deit | |
| And by thi rycht hand yaldin forth my sprete | |
| Quhar that the valiant Hectour losit the swete | *life* |
| On Achillis speir, and grisly Sarpedon, | |
| And ondyr flude Symois mony one | |
| With scheld and helm stalwart bodeis lyis warpit?" | *wrapped* |
| And al invane thus quhil Eneas carpit, | *spoke* |
| A blastrand bub out from the north brayng | *squall* |
| Gan our the forschip in the baksaill dyng, | *strike* |
| And to the sternys up the flude gan cast. | |
| The aris, hechis and the takillis brast, | *oars: hatches: broke* |
| The shippis stevin frawart hyr went gan wryth, | *prow: away from: twisted* |
| And turnyt hir braid syde to the wallis swyth. | *waves: at once* |
| Heich as a hill the jaw of watir brak | *swell* |
| And in ane hepe cam on thame with a swak. | *violent blow* |
| Sum hesit hoverand on the wallis hycht, | *hoisted* |
| And sum the swowchand sey so law gart lycht | *whistling* |
| Thame semyt the erd oppynnyt amyd the flude — | *opened* |
| The stour up bullyrrit sand as it war wode. | *storm: bubbled* |
| The sowth wynd, Nothus, thre schippis draif away | |
| Amang blynd cragis, quhilk huge rolkis thai say | |
| Amyd the sey Italianys Altaris callis; | |
| And othir thre Eurus from the deip wallis | |
| Cachit amang the schald bankis of sand — | *shallows* |
| Dolorus to se thame chop on grond, and stand | *strike* |
| Lyke as a wall with sand warpit about. | |
| Ane othir, in quham salit the Lycianys stowt, | |
| Quhilum fallowis to Kyng Pandor in weir, | *war* |
| And Orontes, Eneas fallow deir, | *companion* |
| Befor his eyn from the north wynd | |

Ane hydduus sey schippit at hir stern behynd,          *shipped*
Smate furth the skippar clepit Lewcaspis,
His hed doune warpit, and the schip with this
Thrys thar the flude quhirlit about round,
The swokand swelth sank under sey and drond.          *gulping whirlpool*
On the huge deip quhoyn salaris dyd appeir;          *few*
The Trojanys armour, takillis and othir geir
Flet on the wallis; and the strang barge tho          *floated*
Bair Ilioneus, and scho that bair also
Forcy Achates, and scho that bair Abas,
And scho quharin ancyant Alethes was,          *old*
The storm ourset, raif rovis and syde semmys —          *tore apart plates*
Thai all lekkit, the salt watir stremmys          *leaked*
Fast bullerand in at every ryft and boyr.          *chink*

Translated from the Latin
by Gavin Douglas (c1474-1522)

## *From* The Shipwreck

Fair Candia now no more beneath her lee
Protects the vessel from the insulting sea;
Round her broad arms, impatient of control,
Roused from the secret deep, the billows roll:
Sunk were the bulwarks of the friendly shore,
And all the scene a hostile aspect wore.
The flattering wind, that late with promised aid
From Candia's bay the unwilling ship betrayed,
No longer fawns beneath the fair disguise,
But like a ruffian on his quarry flies:
Tossed on the tide, she feels the tempest blow,
And dreads the vengeance of so fell a foe —
As the proud horse, with costly trappings gay,
Exulting, prances to the bloody fray;
Spurning the ground, he glories in his might,

But reels tumultuous in the shock of fight:
Ev'n so, caparisoned in gaudy pride,
The bounding vessel dances on the tide.
    Fierce and more fierce the gathering tempest grew,
South, and by west, the threatening demon blew:
The ship no longer can her top-sails spread,
And every hope of fairer skies is fled.
Bow-lines and halyards are cast off again,
Clue-lines hauled down, and sheets let fly amain:
Embrailed each top-sail, and by braces squared,
The seamen climb aloft and man each yard:
They furled the sails, and pointed to the wind
The yards, by rolling tackles then confined,
While o'er the ship the gallant boatswain flies;
Like a hoarse mastiff through the storm he cries.
Prompt to direct the unskilful still appears,
The expert he praises, and the timid cheers.
Now some, to strike top-gallant-yards attend,
Some, travellers up the weather-back-stays send,
At each mast-head the top-ropes others bend.
The parrels, lifts, and clue-lines soon are gone,
Topped and unrigged they down the back-stays run;
The yards secure along the booms were laid,
And all the flying ropes aloft belayed.
Their sails reduced, and all the rigging clear,
Awhile the crew relax from toils severe;
Awhile, their spirits with fatigue oppressed,
In vain expect the alternate hour of rest —
But with redoubling force the tempests blow,
And watery hills in dread succession flow:
A dismal shade o'ercasts the frowning skies,
New troubles grow, new difficulties rise;
No season this from duty to descend!—
"All hands on deck" must now the storm attend.

William Falconer (1732-1769)

# *From* A Saturday's Expedition

At that sweet period of revolving time
When Phoebus lingers not in Thetis' lap;
When twinkling stars their feeble influence shed,
And scarcely glimmer thro' th' ethereal vault,
Till Sol again his near approach proclaims,
With ray purpureal, and the blushing form
Of fair Aurora, goddess of the dawn,
Leading the winged coursers to the pole
Of Phoebus' car: — 'Twas in that season fair,
When jocund Summer did the meads array
In Flora's ripening bloom, that we prepared
To break the bond of business, and to roam
Far from Edina's jarring noise a while.

Fair smiled the wakening morn on our design;
And we, with joy elate, our march began
For Leith's fair port, where oft Edina's sons
The week conclude, and in carousal quaff
Port, punch, rum, brandy, and Geneva strong,
Liquors too nervous for the feeble purse.
With all convenient speed we there arrived:
Nor had we time to touch at house or hall,
Till from the boat a hollow thundering voice
Bellowed vociferous, and our ears assailed
With, "Ho! Kinghorn, oho! come straight aboard."
We failed not to obey the stern command,
Uttered with voice as dreadful as the roar
Of Polyphemus, 'midst rebounding rocks,
When overcome by sage Ulysses' wiles.

"Hoist up your sails," the angry skipper cries,
While fore and aft the busy sailors run,
And lose th' entangled cordage. — O'er the deep
Zephyrus blows, and hugs our lofty sails,
Which, in obedience to the powerful breeze,
Swell o'er the foaming main, and kiss the wave.

Now o'er the convex surface of the flood
Precipitate we fly. Our foaming prow
Divides the saline stream. On either side
Ridges of yesty surge dilate apace;
But from the poop the waters gently flow,
And undulation for the time decays,
In eddies smoothly floating o'er the main.

Here let the Muse in doleful numbers sing
The woeful fate of those, whose cruel stars
Have doom'd them subject to the languid powers
Of watery sickness. — Tho' with stomach full
Of juicy beef, of mutton in its prime,
Or all the dainties Luxury can boast,
They brave the elements, — yet the rocking bark,
Truly regardless of their precious food,
Converts their visage to the ghastly pale,
And makes the sea partaker of the sweets
On which they sumptuous fared. — And this the cause
Why those of Scotia's sons, whose wealthy store
Hath blessed them with a splendid coach and six,
Rather incline to linger on the way,
And cross the river Forth by Stirling Bridge,
Than be subjected to the ocean's swell,
To dangerous ferries, and to sickness dire.

And now at equal distance shews the land. —
Gladly the tars the joyful task pursue
Of gathering in the freight. — Debates arise
From counterfeited halfpence. — In the hold
The seamen scrutinize, and eager peep
Thro' every corner where their watchful eye
Suspects a lurking place, or dark retreat,
To hide the timid corpse of some poor soul,
Whose scanty purse can scarce one groat afford.

At length, we, cheerful, land on Fifan shore,
Where sickness vanishes, and all the ills
Attendant on the passage of Kinghorn.

Our pallid cheeks resume their rosy hue,
And empty stomachs keenly crave supply.
With eager step we reached the friendly inn;
Nor did we think of beating our retreat
'Till every gnawing appetite was quelled.

Robert Fergusson (1750-1774)

# Rule Britannia

When Britain first, at heaven's command,
   Arose from out the azure main,
This was the charter of the land,
   And guardian angels sang this strain.
"Rule, Britannia, rule the waves:
Britons never will be slaves."

The nations not so blest as thee
   Must in their turns to tyrants fall;
While thou shalt flourish great and free,
   The dread and envy of them all.
Rule, Britannia, rule the waves:
Britons never will be slaves.

Still more majestic shalt thou rise,
   More dreadful from each foreign stroke:
As the loud blast that tears the skies
   Serves but to root thy native oak.
Rule, Britannia, rule the waves:
Britons never will be slaves.

Thee haughty tyrants ne'er shall tame:
   All their attempts to bend thee down
Will but arouse thy generous flame —
   But work their woe and thy renown.
Rule, Britannia, rule the waves:
Britons never will be slaves.

To thee belongs the rural reign;
    Thy cities shall with commerce shine;
All thine shall be the subject main,
    And every shore it circles thine.
Rule, Britannia, rule the waves:
Britons never will be slaves.

The Muses, still with freedom found,
    Shall to thy happy coast repair.
Blest isle! with matchless beauty crowned,
    And manly hearts to guard the fair.
Rule, Britannia, rule the waves:
Britons never will be slaves.

David Mallet (c1705-1765)

# The Lowlands of Holland

My love he's built a bonnie ship, and set her on the sea,
With seven score guid mariners to bear her companie.
There's three score is sunk, and three score dead at sea;
And the lowlands of Holland hae twined my love and me.

My love he built another ship, and set her on the main,
And nane but twenty mariners for to bring her hame;
But the weary wind began to rise, and the sea began to rout,
My love then, and his bonnie ship, turned withershins about.

There shall neither coif come on my head, nor kame come in my hair;
There shall neither coal nor candle-licht come in my bower mair;
Nor will I love another man until the day I dee,
For I never loved a love but ane, and he's drown'd in the sea.

O haud your tongue, my daughter dear, be still and be content;
There are mair lads in Galloway, ye need na sair lament.
O! there is nane in Galloway, there's nane at a' for me;
For I never loved a love but ane, and he's drown'd in the sea.

# *From* The Birlinn of Clanranald

*A man was set apart for the tackle.*

Let a broad man, stout and brawny,
　　By the rigging sit:
One who with care will keep firm hold
　　As doth befit;
Who the end of the yard arm
　　Will downward press,
And mast and tackle will relieve
　　In time of stress;
Who knows the breeze as it comes on,
　　Its course to meet;
Answering steadily the pull
　　Of the man at the sheet;
With the tackle ever helping,
Lest the stout and hairy rigging
　　Should ever fail.

Alexander Macdonald (c1700-c1780)
Translated from the Gaelic
by Rev. A. and Rev. A. Macdonald

# Sea Prayer

| | |
|---|---|
| *Helmsman:* | Blest be the boat. |
| *Crew:* | God the Father bless her. |
| | Blest be the boat. |
| | God the Son bless her. |
| | Blest be the boat. |
| | God the Spirit bless her. |
| *All:* | God the Father. |
| | God the Son, |
| | God the Spirit, |
| |    Bless the boat. |
| *Helmsman:* | What can befall you |
| | And God the Father with you? |
| *Crew:* | No harm can befall us. |
| | What can befall you |
| | And God the Son with you? |
| | No harm can befall us. |
| | What can befall you |
| | And God the Spirit with you? |
| | No harm can befall us. |
| *All:* | God the Father, |
| | God the Son, |
| | God the Spirit, |
| |    With us eternally. |
| *Helmsman:* | What can cause you anxiety |
| | And the God of the elements over you? |
| *Crew:* | No anxiety can be ours. |
| | What can cause you anxiety |
| | And the King of the elements over you? |
| | No anxiety can be ours. |
| | What can cause you anxiety |
| | And the Spirit of the elements over you? |
| | No anxiety can be ours. |

*All:* The God of the elements,
The King of the elements,
The Spirit of the elements,
Close over us,
    Ever eternally.

Translated from the Gaelic
by Alexander Carmichael

# *Food and Drink*

*That the Scots subsist on whisky and haggis is as much a part of internat-ional food-lore as that the French eat little but snails and frogs' legs and the Germans exist on lager and sausage. Be that as it may, Burns' encomium on the haggis seems to be the only poem on that delicacy; and though much whisky was distilled (a lot of it illegally) and drunk in the 18th century, the considerable literature on that subject does not begin until later.*

*Possibly the earliest meal in Scottish literature is that taken by Charle-magne in the medieval alliterative poem Rauf Coilyear, at which brawn of boar, capon, rabbit and "birds baked in bread" are on the menu. Rauf the Collier and his wife Gill, or Gyliane, who does the serving, do not know the identity of their guest, who has lost his way in the forest in a storm while out hunting.*

*In fact, until about the beginning of the 18th century, the fare of the great majority of Scots was basic and sparse: if the French connection influenced eating habits at Court and, to a lesser extent, among the upper classes who copied court manners, it had no effect on the rural and urban poor, who made do with oatmeal, turnips and kale. Indeed kale, or kail, came to be synonymous with "dinner", as in:*

> *The monks o' Melrose made guid kale.*
> *On Fridays when they fasted;*
> *Nor wanted they guid beef and ale*
> *As lang's their neighbour's lasted.*

*Whatever kind of beef the monks may have had, for some centuries the diet of the majority was varied only by the most unappetising of meat, or by her-ring for people who lived by the coast. Predictably, these staples of diet did not inspire much literature, and it is significant that Caller Herrin', with its sentimental appeal on behalf of the fisher-folk, was written by a Baroness. "Caller" is Scots for "fresh", by the way.*

*However, Caller Oysters reminds us that these Scottish molluscs were* once accessible to many. Scotland's Mrs Beeton, Mistress Margaret Dods (the pseudonym of Isobel Christian Johnston, 1781-1857), wrote: "The principal taverns of our Old City used to be called Oyster-Taverns, in honour of their favourite viand." Fergusson refers in his poem to eating oysters in "Luckie (i.e. the female keeper of an ale-house) Middlemist's". Another famous Edinburgh "landlady" was Lucky Wood, whose passing, and whose hospitality, Ramsay mourns. Mourning is the key-note, too, of the sad ballad of Lord Donald, though one hastens to add that the native fare that appears to have killed him was not fish, but toads.

Brewing is one of Scotland's oldest industries — laws governing the establishment of brew-houses were enacted in the time of William the Lion, 1165-1214. However, for some centuries, ale was privately brewed and sold, as we learn from "Wha Hes Gud Malt", by ale-wives. While Duncan Ban MacIntyre's rollicking drinking song reminds us that in the 18th century a "dram" could as easily mean a measure of brandy as of whisky.

# To a Haggis

Fair fa' your honest sonsie face,
Great chieftain o' the puddin'-race!
Aboon them a' ye tak your place,
   Painch, tripe, or thairm:
Weel are ye wordy o' a grace
   As lang's my arm.

The groaning trencher there ye fill,
Your hurdies like a distant hill;
Your pin wad help to mend a mill
   In time o'need;
While thro' your pores the dews distil
   Like amber bead.

His knife see rustic Labour dight,
An' cut you up wi' ready sleight,
Trenching your gushing entrails bright
   Like ony ditch;
And then, O what a glorious sight
   Warm-reekin', rich!

Then, horn for horn they stretch an' strive,
Deil tak the hindmost! on they drive,
Till a' their weel-swall'd kytes belyve
   Are bent like drums;
Then auld guidman, maist like to rive,
   Bethankit hums.

Is there that o'er his French ragout,
Or olio that wad staw a sow,
Or fricassee wad mak her spew
   Wi' perfect sconner,
Looks down wi' sneering scornfu' view
   On sic a dinner?

Poor devil! see him owre his trash,
As feckless as a wither'd rash,
His spindle shank a guid whip-lash,
    His nieve a nit:
Thro' bloody flood or field to dash.
    O how unfit!

But mark the Rustic, haggis-fed —
The trembling earth resounds his tread!
Clap in his walie nieve a blade,
    He'll mak it whissle;
An' legs, an' arms, an' heads will sned,
    Like taps o' thrissle.

Ye Pow'rs, wha mak mankind your care,
And dish them out their bill o' fare,
Auld Scotland wants nae skinking ware
    That jaups in luggies;
But, if ye wish her gratefu' prayer,
    Gie her a Haggis!

Robert Burns (1759-1796)

## *From* Rauf Coilyear

Quhen thay war seruit and set to the Suppar,
Gyll and the gentill King, Charlis of micht,
Syne on the tother syde sat the Coilyear:                    *then: collier*
Thus war thay marschellit but mair, and matchit that nicht.  *placed*
Thay brocht breid to the buird, and braun of ane bair,       *boar*
And the worthyest wyne went vpon hicht;
Thay Beirnis, as I wene, thay had aneuch thair,              *knights*
Within that burelie bigging, byrnand full bricht;            *strong house*
Syne enteris thair daynteis on deis dicht dayntelie.         *table: prepared*
    Within that worthie wane                                 *dwelling*
    Forsuith wantit thay nane.
    With blyith cheir sayis Gyliane:
        "Schir, dois glaidlie."

The Carll carpit to the King cumlie and cleir:  *spoke*
"Schir, the Forestaris, forsuith, of this Forest,
Thay haue me all at Inuy for dreid of the Deir;  *spite: are afraid for*
Thay threip that I thring doun of the fattest;  *maintain: kill*
Thay say, I sall to Paris, thair to compeir  *appear*
Befoir our cumlie King, in dule to be drest;  *to be dealt with*
Sic manassing thay me mak, forsuith, ilk yeir,  *menacing*
And yit aneuch sall I haue for me and ane Gest;
Thairfoir sic as thow seis, spend on, and not spair."
   Thus said gentill Charlis the Mane
   To the Coilyear agane:
   "The King him self hes bene fane  *glad*
     Sum tyme of sic fair."

Of Capounis and Cunningis thay had plentie,  *rabbits*
With wyne at thair will, and eik Vennysoun;
Byrdis bakin in breid, the best that may be;
Thus full freschlie thay fure into fusioun.  *fared: plenty*
The Carll with ane cleir voce carpit on he,
Said: "Gyll, lat the cop raik for my bennysoun;  *cup: proceed: toast*
And gar our Gaist begin, and syne drink thow to me;
Sen he is ane stranger, me think it ressoun."
Thay drank dreichlie about, thay wosche, and thay rais.  *deeply: in turn*
   The King with ane blyith cheir
   Thankit the Coilyeir;
   Syne all the thre into feir
     To the fyre gais.

(Late 15th Century)

# Caller Herrin'

Wha'll buy my caller herrin'?
 They're bonnie fish and halesome farin';
Wha'll buy my caller herrin',
 New drawn frae the Forth?

When ye were sleepin' on your pillows,
 Dream'd ye aught o' our puir fellows,
Darkling as they fac'd the billows,
 A' to fill the woven willows?
  Buy my caller herrin',
  New drawn frae the Forth.

Wha'll buy my caller herrin'?
 They're no brought here without brave darin';
Buy my caller herrin',
 Haul'd thro' wind and rain.
  Wha'll buy my caller herrin'? etc.

Wha'll buy my caller herrin'?
 Oh, ye may ca' them vulgar farin' —
Wives and mithers, maist despairin',
 Ca' them lives o' men.
  Wha'll buy my caller herrin'? etc.

When the creel o' herrin' passes,
 Ladies, clad in silks and laces,
Gather in their braw pelisses,
 Cast their heads and screw their faces.
  Wha'll buy my caller herrin'? etc.

Caller herrin 's no got lightlie: —
 Ye can trip the spring fu' tightlie;
Spite o' tauntin', flauntin', flingin',
 Gow has set you a' a-singing
  Wha'll buy my caller herrin'? etc.

Neebour wives, now tent my tellin':
    When the bonnie fish ye're sellin',
At ae word be in yere dealin' —
    Truth will stand when a' thing 's failin',
        Wha'll buy my caller herrin'?
    They're bonnie fish and halesome farin',
    Wha'll buy my caller herrin',
        New drawn frae the Forth?

Lady Nairne (1766-1845)

# ■ Caller Oysters

O' a' the waters that can hobble,
A fishing yole or sa'mon coble,
And can reward the fisher's trouble,
    Or south or north,
There's nane sae spacious and sae noble,
    As Firth o' Forth.

In her the skate and codlin sail;
The eel, fu' souple, wags her tail;
Wi' herrin, fleuk, and mackarel,
    And whytens dainty:
Their spindleshanks the labsters trail,
    Wi' partans plenty.

Auld Reikie's sons blythe faces wear;
September's merry month is near,
That brings in Neptune's caller cheer,
    New oysters fresh;
The halesomest and nicest gear
    O' fish or flesh.

O! then we needna gie a plack
For dand'ring mountebank or quack,
Wha o' their drogs sae bauldly crack,
    An' spread sic notions,
As gar their feckless patients tak
    Their stinking potions.

Come, prie, frail man! for gin thou art sick,
The oyster is a rare cathartic,
As ever doctor patient gart lick,
    To cure his ails;
Whether you hae the head or heart-ake,
    It ay prevails.

Ye tipplers, open a' your poses:
Ye, wha are fash'd wi' plouky noses,
Fling o'er your craig sufficient doses;
    You'll thole a hunder,
To fleg awa your simmer roses,
    And naething under.

Whan big as burns the gutters rin,
Gin ye hae catcht a droukit skin,
To luckie Middlemist's loup in,
    And sit fu' snug
Owre oysters and a dram o' gin,
    Or haddock lug.

Whan auld Saunt Giles, at eight o'clock,
Gars merchant lowns their shopies lock,
There we adjourn wi' hearty fouk
    To birle our bodles,
And get wharewi' to crack our joke,
    And clear our noddles.

Whan Phoebus did his winnocks steek,
How aften at that ingle cheek
Did I my frosty fingers beek,
    And prie good fare?
I trow there was nae hame to seek,
    Whan steghin there.

While glaikit fools, owre rife o' cash,
Pamper their wames wi' fousom trash,
I think a chiel may gayly pass,
    He's nae ill bodden,
That gusts his gab wi' oyster sauce,
    An' hen weel sodden.

At Musselbrough, and eke Newhaven,
The fisher wives will get top livin'
Whan lads gang out on Sunday's even
    To treat their joes,
And tak o' fat pandores a prievin',
    Or mussel brose.

Then, sometimes, ere they flit their doup,
They'll aiblins a' their siller coup
For liquor clear, frae cutty stoup,
    To weet their wizzen,
And swallow owre a dainty soup,
    For fear they gizzen.

A' ye wha canna stand sae sicker,
Whan twice ye've toom'd the big-ars'd bicker,
Mix cauler oysters wi' your liquor,
    And I'm your debtor,
If greedy priest or drowthy vicar
    Will thole it better.

Robert Fergusson (1750-1774)

# Elegy on Lucky Wood in the Canongate, May 1717

O *Canningate!* poor elritch Hole,
What Loss, what Crosses does thou thole!
*London* and Death gars thee look drole,
   And hing thy Head;
Wow, but thou has e'en a cauld Coal
    To blaw indeed.

Hear me ye Hills, and every Glen,
Ilk Craig, ilk Cleugh, and hollow Den,
And Echo shrill, that a' may ken
   The waefou Thud,
Be rackless Death, wha came unsenn
    To Lucky *Wood.*

She's dead o'er true, she's dead and gane,
Left us and *Willie* Burd alane,
To bleer and greet, to sob and mane,
   And rugg our Hair,
Because we'll ne'r see her again
    For evermair.

She gae'd as fait as a new Prin,
And kept her Housie snod and been;
Her Peuther glanc'd upo' your Een
   Like Siller Plate;
She was a donsie Wife and clean,
    Without Debate.

It did ane good to see her Stools,
Her Boord, Fire-side, and facing Tools;
Rax, Chandlers, Tangs, and Fire-Shools,
   Basket wi' Bread.
Poor Facers now may chew Pea-hools,
    Since Lucky's dead.

She ne'er gae in a Lawin fause,
Nor Stoups a Froath aboon the Hause,
Nor kept dow'd Tip within her Waw's,
    But reaming Swats;
She never ran sour Jute, because
    It gee's the Batts.

She had the Gate sae well to please,
With *gratis* Beef, dry Fish, or Cheese;
Which kept our Purses ay at Ease,
    And Health in Tift,
And lent her fresh Nine Gallon Trees
    A hearty Lift.

She ga'e us aft hail Legs o' Lamb,
And did nae hain her Mutton Ham;
Than ay at *Yule*, when e'er we came,
    A bra' Goose Pye,
And was na that good Belly Baum?
    Nane dare deny.

The Writer Lads fow well may mind her,
Furthy was she, her Luck design'd her
Their common Mither, sure nane kinder
    Ever brake Bread;
She has na left her Make behind her,
    But now she's dead.

To the sma' Hours we aft sat still,
Nick'd round our Toasts and Snishing Mill;
Good Cakes we wanted ne'r at Will,
    The best of Bread,
Which aften cost us mony a Gill
    To *Aikenhead*.

Cou'd our saut Tears like *Clyde* down rin,
And had we Cheeks like *Corra's* Lin,
That a' the Warld might hear the Din
    Rair frae ilk Head;
She was the Wale of a' her Kin,
    But now she's dead.

O Lucky *Wood*, 'tis hard to bear
The Loss; but Oh! we maun forbear:
Ye sall thy Memory be dear
    While blooms a Tree,
And after Ages Bairns will spear
    'Bout Thee and Me.

### EPITAPH
*Beneath this Sod*
*Lies Lucky Wood,*
*Whom a' Men might put Faith in;*
    *Wha was na sweer,*
    *While she winn'd here,*
*To cramm our Wames for naithing.*

Allan Ramsay (1684-1758)

# Lord Donald

"Oh, whare ha'e ye been all day, Lord Donald, my son?
Oh, whare ha'e ye been all day, my jolly young man?"
"I've been awa courtin'; mither, make my bed soon,
For I'm sick at the heart, and I fain would lie down."

"What wou'd you ha'e for your supper, Lord Donald, my son?
What wou'd you ha'e for your supper, my jolly young man?"
"I've gotten my supper; mither, make my bed soon,
For I'm sick at the heart, and I fain would lie down."

"What did ye get for your supper, Lord Donald, my son?
What did ye get for your supper, my jolly young man?"
"A dish of sma' fishes; mither, make my bed soon,
For I'm sick at the heart, and I fain would lie down."

"Whare gat ye the fishes, Lord Donald, my son?
Whare gat ye the fishes, my jolly young man?"
"In my father's black ditches; mither, make my bed soon,
For I'm sick at the heart, and I fain would lie down."

"What like were your fishes, Lord Donald, my son?
What like were your fishes, my jolly young man?"
"Black backs and speckl'd bellies; mither, make my bed soon,
For I'm sick at the heart, and I fain would lie down."

"Oh, I fear ye are poison'd, Lord Donald, my son!
Oh, I fear ye are poison'd,  my jolly young man!"
"Oh, yes! I am poison'd; mither, make my bed soon,
For I'm sick at the heart, and I fain would lie down."

"What will you leave to your father, Lord Donald, my son?
What will ye leave to your father, my jolly young man?"
"Baith my houses and land; mither, make my bed soon,
For I'm sick at the heart, and I fain would lie down."

"What will you leave to yeur brither, Lord Donald, my son?
What will ye leave to your brither, my jolly young man?"
"My horse and the saddle; mither, make my bed soon,
For I'm sick at the heart, and I fain would lie down."

"What will you leave to your sister, Lord Donald, my son?
What will ye leave to your sister, my jolly young man?"
"Baith my gold box and rings; mither, make my bed soon,
For I'm sick at the heart, and I fain would lie down."

"What will you leave to your true love, Lord Donald, my son?
What will you leave to your true love, my jolly young man?"
"The tow and the halter, for to hang on yon tree,
And let her hang there for the poisoning of me."

# "Wha Hes Gud Malt"

Wha hes gud malt and makis ill drink,
    Wa mot be hir werd! *woe: destiny*
I pray to God scho rot and stink, *she*
    Sevin yeir abone the erd; *above the ground*
About hir beir na bell to clink,
    Nor clerk sing, lawid nor lerd; *loud: learned*
Bot quite to hell that scho may sink
    The taptre whyll scho steird: *bung: removed*
      This beis my prayer
      For that man sleyar,
    Whill Christ in Hevin sall heird. *until*

Wha brewis and gevis me of the best,
    Sa it be stark and staill, *strong and old*
White and cleir, weill to degest,
    In Hevin meit hir that aill!
Lang mot scho leif, lang mot scho lest
    In lyking ane gude saill; *hall*
In Hevin or erd that wyfe be best,
    Without barrat or bail; *trouble or sorrow*
      When scho is deid,
      Withowtin pleid, *argument*
Scho pass to Hevin all haill. *at once*

# Song to the Brandy

## LAY

*Di-haal-lum, di-haal-lum, di-i'il-i'il, hanndan,*
*Di-dir-ir-i-hal-hi'il-lum, di-dir-ir-i-hal-haoi-rum;*
*Di-i'il-i'il hal-dir-ir-i, ha-ri-ha'al-haoi-rum,*
*Di-i'il-haal-dil-il-i'il, dor-ri-ho'ol-hann-dan.*

There's fortune in't, we'll have a drink,
    Don't let the glass be spared on us,
There's plenty in the bottles' clink,
    Their contents are not wared on us;
We're better of it at the first
    "To kittle up our notion,"
Though we'd all drinks to quench our thirst,
    The Brandy's our best potion.
        *Di-haal-lum, &c.*

That is the fancy-raising brew,
    The lucky well, the sweet one;
There's flavour there and savour to
    Put spirit in a weak man,
The better we of what we want,
    No stuff to set heads ringing,
Right good as a throat lubricant,
    Whoe'er a stave is singing.

The men in whom is jollity,
    Who nothing lack in mettle,
Companions in potation, they
    Down to their dram will settle;
And they will ask it yet again
    Ere it be low, they fancy,
Whene'er they hear the fiddle's strain
    And they would fain be dancing.

When we shall from the barrels get
　　All we wish in our power o' it,
In glasses that are empty set
　　From jars we empty more o' it;
And every friend who's pleasing us
　　We'd wish him speech to bandy,
When round comes the delicious glass
　　With the taste of sugar-candy.

We're in no danger that it fail,
　　There's cellars-full in France o' it;
There is no fear of want o' it near
　　The shipping that it thence brought:
And since we like it well, we'll say it,
　　'Tis not its fault will worst us;
The longer that we for it wait,
　　The more intense our thirst is.

The men that are so niggardly
　　Won't spend their share to match us,
Along with us they must not be,
　　The poverty-struck wretches:
They don't seek into company,
　　The company don't want them;
Useless the burn their thirst allay,
　　They'd never get the quantum.

Duncan Ban MacIntyre (1724-1812)
Translated from the Gaelic
by George Carter

# Sport and Entertainment

*One's first impression from the pieces which follow is that some sports have hardly changed down the centuries. Footballers still suffer fractures and torn muscles, and broken homes are a common hazard among sportsmen. Duncan Ban MacIntyre's* On Missing at Hunting *perfectly epitomises the joy of the chase rather than the kill. While James Fisher's description of a curling match outdoors would be as valid today as it was then — and it is an even more vivid report in that Fisher was blind.*

*However, sport was originally not for peasants — even the archery contest so hilariously parodied in* Christ's Kirk on the Grene *would have been performed by members of the upper classes. This is an early example of the Scottish tradition of composing witty, rumbustious poems about popular events and festivals — Robert Fergusson wrote one some two hundred years later on Leith Races; Burns wrote in a similar vein on Hallow Fair. Allan Ramsay might be nominated as the first sports' journalist, as his* Leith Races *first appeared in the Caledonian Mercury of 2 August 1736. Fergusson's* Elegy on the Death of Scots Music *is notable not so much for its sentiments as for the fact that it was one of the first of his poems to be published that was written in Scots. His earlier, and less-distinguished, efforts had been pastoral poems in the English style.*

*The theatre in Scotland in the 18th century was under continuous threat — at one time or another almost every theatre in Glasgow was burned down, either accidentally or by religious fanatics who felt that theatres were houses of the Devil. But still, new theatres opened, and Ramsay was often called upon to write a prologue for such an event. The one quoted here is included for its historical interest rather than its poetic quality. The theatre was a private house in Carrubber's Close. The following year, the Society of High Constables, of which Ramsay was a member, tried to "suppress the abominable stage-plays lately set up by Anthony Alston". The Canongate Theatre whose ruin Fergusson contemplates was opened in 1747, and was run by a good English company under the debt-prone actor-manager West Digges. It was here that the first performance took place in*

1756 of John Home's "Douglas", which is said to have moved one of the audience to cry, "Whaur's your Wullie Shakespeare noo?" However, the opening of the Theatre Royal at the fashionable New Town end of the North Bridge in 1769 proved the end of the Canongate Theatre.

## "The Bewteis of the Fute-Ball"

| | |
|---|---|
| Brissit brawnis and broken banis | *torn muscles* |
| Strife, discord and wastit wanis, | *broken homes* |
| Crookit in eild, syne halt withal — | *old age* |
| Thir are the bewteis of the fute-ball. | |

From the Maitland Folio (16th century)

## *From* A Winter Season

With tramps, and brooms, and stones, a crowd now comes,
The long-projected curling-match to try,
For beef and greens, and something else beside,
To cheer the heart, which makes the tongue oft boast
Of great achievements on the ice perform'd;
Exciting still fresh challenges to play
That king of games, best cordial for the nerves.
From Solway's firth, to where the mighty Forth,
By curious windings, vainly seeks to shun
His contributions to the German sea:
A game much us'd, but scarcely ever known
Beyond their bounds, in either South or North.
The rink now chosen out, and distance fix'd,
The tees both made, and hog-scores justly drawn,
The best of three, nine, or eleven shot games,
Agreed upon, the dinner to decide;
A piece of coin is then toss'd high in air
To show which side shall first begin the sport,
Or, not so heathenish, this perhaps to know,
A stone is played by one upon each side;
And now the keen contested match begins.
Stones roar from tee to tee the ice along,
Lie here, — strike this, — well done, — guard that, — well play'd,
Alternate cry, those who the game direct.

Soon as a stone the hog-score o'er has got,
And judg'd by those concern'd to stop too short,
Sweep, sweep! O haste and sweep, then's all the cry,
How then the brooms are ply'd to sweep it on!
But when the distance-score one does not reach,
'Tis hog it off, with laughter much and loud:
And still the cheering, healthful sport goes on,
Till three huzzas declare the victor side;
Now off they go, with appetite to dine,
And spend, in social glee, the evening all.

James Fisher (born 1759)

# *From* Christ's Kirk on the Grene

| | |
|---|---|
| Than Robene Roy begouth to revell, | *began* |
| And Dowie to him druggit; | |
| "Lat be!" quod Johke, and callit him gavell, | *rascal* |
| And be the taill him tuggit; | |
| He turnit and cleikit to the cavell, | *hooked on: rude fellow* |
| Bot Lord than gif thai luggit! | *how: pulled* |
| Thai partit thair play thane with ane nevell | *wallop* |
| Men wait gif hair wes ruggit | *know: torn out* |
| Betwene thame | |
| At Chrystis Kirk on the grein. | |

| | |
|---|---|
| Ane bend ane bow, sic sturt couth steir him; | *fighting* |
| Grit scayth war to have scard him; | *loss* |
| He chesit ane flaine as did affeir him; | *arrow: frighten* |
| The tother said "Dirdum Dardum!" | |
| Throw bayth the cheikis he thocht to cheir him, | *pierce* |
| Or throw the chaftis have charde him | *jaws* |
| Bot be ane myle it come nocht neir him. | |
| I can nocht say quhat mard him | |
| Thair | |
| At Chrystis Kirk on the grein. | |

With that ane freynd of his cryit, "Fy!"
And up ane arow drew,
He forgeit it so ferslye                                    *bent*
The bow in flenders flew;
Sa was the will of God, trow I;
For had the tre bent trew,
Men said that kend his archerie
That he had slane anew
That day
At Chrystis Kirk on the grein.

Ane haistie hensour callit Harie                           *spark*
Quhilk wes ane archer heynd,                               *young*
Tit up ane takill but ony tarye,                          *took: weapon*
That turment so him teynd;                                 *angry*
I wait nocht quhidder his hand cud varie,
Or gif the man was his freynd
Bot he chapit throw the michtis of Marie                   *escaped*
As man that na evill meynd
That tyme
At Chrystis Kirk on the grein.

Than Lowrie as ane lyoun lap
And sone ane flane culd fedder;                             *feather*
He hecht to pers him at the pape,                          *promised: breast*
Thairon to wed ane wedder;                                *bet: ram*
He hit him on the wambe ane wap,                          *belly*
And it bust lyk ane bledder;
But lo! as fortoun was and hap,
His doublat was of ledder
And sauft him
At Chrystis Kirk on the grein.

The baff so boustuousle abasit him,                        *roughly*
To the erd he duschit doun;
The tother for dreid he preissit him
And fled out of the toun;
The wyffis come furth and up thay paisit him               *lifted*
And fand lyff in the loun

And with thre routis thay raisit him     *cheers*
And coverit him of swoune     *resuscitated*
Agane
At Chrystis Kirk on the grein.

Ane yaip young man that stude him neist     *keen*
Lousit of ane schot with ire;
He etlit the berne evin in the breist,     *aimed at: man*
The bout flew our the byre;
Ane cryit that he had slane ane preist
Ane myle beyond ane myre;
Than bow and bag fra him he caist,
And fled als fers as fyre
Of flint
At Chrystis Kirk on the grein.

(Late 15th century)

# ■ Song on Missing at Hunting

> *I saw the dun stag and the hinds*
> *Ascending the pass together:*
> *I saw the dun stag and the hinds.*

I'm down from Misty Corrie trailing,
    Great's my chagrin and joyless me;
I fired the shot me not availing,
    Treading all day the forest free.
    *I saw the dun stag and the hinds, etc.*

Though upon arms is laid a veto,
    I kept the Spaniard for the hill,
Despite the trick she treated me to,
    The son o' the hind she failed to kill.

Up in the morning I at once got,
    In her I put Glasgow powder,
A tight ball, three English swan-shot,
    Then with wad of tow I stowed her.

Fresh the flint was on renewing,
    And oil I put into the spring,
A skin-case was, for fear of dewing,
    On my companion ward keeping.

The hind, she lay down by the well,
    And I went round about her easy,
Let off at her yon shot so fell —
    That she arose, it did not please me.

The side of the steep bank I won,
    At her my charge of lead I spent it;
And when I thought she was undone,
    That was the time she highest sprinted.

'Tis sad to be in forest gone
    In day of wind when rain-floods rattle —
Strict orders to seek venison
    The hunters putting on their mettle.

To the glens 'tis high time to go down,
    Since on the peaks there's gloomy plight,
And mists closed in the hills around,
    A blindness causing on our sight.

That next day better will befall us
    We shall live in best of hopes,
That wind, sun, landscape will be all as
    We desire upon the slopes.

Grey lead will fly in lightning flood,
    To clean-flanked dogs a smooth course clear;
And the dun stag is dripping blood,
    And to the active men good cheer.

Duncan Ban MacIntyre (1724-1812)
Translated from the Gaelic
by George Carter

# Leith Races

His Majesty, Heaven guide His Grace,
Encourages each Year a Race
Upon *Leith-sands;* where, at Laigh Tide,
A Million may uncrowded ride:
And the *Good Town*, to mend the Play,
Maintains the Sport another Day.
The sprightly Lads from far and near
In their best Airs and Looks appear,
Dress'd in their easy Hunting Weeds,
Well mounted on their mettled Steeds;
While from the Chariot, or the Green,
A shining Circle charms our Een,
Whose ev'ry Glance emits a Dart
Whops whizzing thro' the stoutest Heart.
Ye Men of Rowth, ne'er hain your Treasure,
For any thing may give Them Pleasure,
And since they like to show their Faces
At *Plays, Assemblies,* and *Horse-Races,*
Support these Interviews of Love,
Which Men of clearest Heads approve,
Rather than waste your Wealth at Cards
Or blast your Health with drunken Lairds.
Ah, ne'er let manly Pastime dwine,
For sake of either Dice or Wine;
But keep a Groom can rightly nurse
The *shapely Racer* for the *Course,*
That, barring some unseen Mischance,
The Master's Honour may advance,
While loud o'er the extended Sands
The Crowd rejoice and clap their Hands.
Should we endure the taunting Tales
Of *Hunters* on *Northumber's* dales,
While o'er their Tankards of brown Stout,
They at our careless gentry flout —
"Come *Dick* ! says *Harry*, mount your Gray,
   I'll bett against you on my Bay:
   Let's down to *Leith* — we're sure to win,

Where there's no better Nags to run.
Of two rich Plates their *Gazette* tells,
For which they keep no Horse themsells.
Since we so cheap may gain each Cup,
We'll e'en step down and bring them up."
Well, this had been just now our Case,
Had not Sir James join'd in the Race,
Whose *Bonny Lass* of *Livingston,*
Defeat *Cutlugs* and *Judy* Brown.
Thanks to the *Knight* who props our Game.
O! may his Coursers ne'er prove lame,
But ever 'gainst the Day design'd
Be able to outfly the Wind
And every Year bring him a Prize
'Till Heaps on Heaps the Trophies rise.

Allan Ramsay (1684-1758)

# Elegy on the Death of Scots Music

On Scotia's plains, in days of yore,
When lads and lasses tartan wore,
Saft Music rang on ilka shore,
    In hamely weed;
But Harmony is now no more,
    And Music dead.

Round her the feather'd choir wad wing,
Sae bonnily she wont to sing,
And sleely wake the sleeping string,
    Their sang to lead,
Sweet as the zephyrs of the spring;
    But now she's dead.

Mourn ilka nymph and ilka swain,
Ilk sunny hill and dowie glen;
Let weeping streams and Naiads drain
    Their fountain head;
Let Echo swell the dolefu' strain,
    Since Music's dead.

Whan the saft vernal breezes ca'
The grey-hair'd Winter's fogs awa',
Naebody then is heard to blaw,
    Near hill or mead,
On chaunter, or on aiten straw,
    Since Music's dead.

Nae lasses now, on simmer days,
Will lilt at bleaching o' their claes;
Nae herds on Yarrow's bonny braes,
    Or banks o' Tweed,
Delight to chant their hameil lays,
    Since Music's dead.

At gloamin now the bagpipe's dumb,
Whan weary owsen hameward come;
Sae sweetly as it wont to bum,
    And pibrachs skreed;
We never hear its warlike hum;
    For Music's dead.

Macgibbon's gane: Ah! waes my heart!
The man in Music maist expert,
Wha could sweet melody impart,
    And tune the reed,
Wi' sic a slee and pawky art;
    But now he's dead.

Ilk carline now may grunt and grane,
Ilk bonny lassie mak great mane,
Since he's awa', I trow there's nane
    Can fill his stead;
The blithest sangster on the plain!
    Alake, he's dead!

Now foreign sonnets bear the gree,
And crabbed queer variety
Of sounds fresh sprung frae Italy,
    A bastard breed!
Unlike that saft-tongu'd melody
    Which now lies dead.

Could lav'rocks at the dawning day,
Could linties chirming frae the spray,
Or todling burns that smocthly play
    O'er gowden bed,
Compare wi' Birks of Invermay?
    But now they're dead.

O Scotland! that could aince afford
To bang the pith of Roman sword,
Winna your sons, wi' joint accord,
    To battle speed?
And fight till Music be restor'd,
    Which now lies dead.

Robert Fergusson (1750-1774)

# Prologue Spoken by Mr Anthony Alston, 1726

'Tis I, — dear *Caledonians*, blythsome *TONY*,
That oft, last Winter, pleas'd the Brave and Bonny
With Medley, merry Song, and comick Scene;
Your Kindness *then* has brought me here again:
After a Circuit round the Queen of Isles,
To gain your Friendship and approving Smiles,
Experience bids me hope; — tho' South the *Tweed*
The Dastards said, "He never will succeed:
"What! such a Country look for any Good in!
"That does not relish Plays, — nor Pork, — nor Pudding!"
Thus great *Columbus* by an Idiot Crew
Was ridicul'd, at first, for his just View;
Yet his undaunted Spirit ne'er gave Ground,
Till he a new and *better* World had found.
So I — laugh on — the Simile is bold;
But Faith 'tis just: For till this Body's cold,
*Columbus* like, I'll push for Fame and Gold.

Allan Ramsay (1684-1758)

# The Canongate Playhouse in Ruins

Ye few, whose feeling hearts are ne'er estranged
From soft emotions! ye who often wear
The eye of Pity, and oft vent her sighs,
When sad Melpomene, in woe-fraught strains,
Gains entrance to the breast; or often smile
When brisk Thalia gaily trips along
Scenes of enlivening mirth; attend my song!
And Fancy, thou whose ever-flaming light
Can penetrate into the dark abyss
Of chaos and of hell; O! with thy blazing torch
The wasteful scene illumine, that the Muse
With daring pinions may her flight pursue,
Nor with timidity be known to soar
O'er the theatric world, to chaos changed.

Can I contemplate on those dreary scenes
Of mouldering desolation, and forbid
The voice elegiac, and the falling tear!
No more, from box to box, the basket, piled
With oranges as radiant as the spheres,
Shall with their luscious virtues charm the sense
Of taste and smell. No more the gaudy beau
With handkerchief in lavender well drenched,
Or *bergamot*, or *rose-watero* pure,
With flavoriferous sweets shall chase away
The pestilential fumes of vulgar cits,
Who, in impatience for the curtain's rise,
Amused the lingering moments, and applied
Thirst-quenching porter to their parched lips.

Alas! how sadly altered is the scene!
For, lo! those sacred walls, that late were brushed
By rustling silks and waving capuchines,
Are now become the sport of wrinkled Time!
Those walls, that late have echoed to the voice
Of stern King Richard, to the seat transformed

Of crawling spiders and detested moths,
Who in the lonely crevices reside,
Or gender in the beams, that have upheld
Gods, demi-gods, and all the joyous crew
Of thunderers in the galleries above.

O Shakespeare! where are all thy tinselled kings,
Thy fawning courtiers, and thy waggish clowns?
Where all thy fairies, spirits, witches, fiends,
That here have gambolled in nocturnal sport,
Round the lone oak, or sunk in fear away
From the shrill summons of the cock at morn?
Where now the temples, palaces, and towers?
Where now the groves that ever verdant smiled?
Where now the streams that never ceased to flow?
Where now the clouds, the rains, the hails, the winds,
The thunders, lightnings, and the tempests strong?

Here shepherds, lolling in their woven bowers,
In dull *recitativo* often sung
Their loves, accompanied with clangour strong
From horns, from trumpets, clarinets, bassoons;
From violinos sharp, or droning bass,
Or the brisk tinkling of a harpsichord.

Such is thy power, O Music! such thy fame,
That it has fabled been, how foreign song,
Soft issuing from Tenducci's slender throat,
Has drawn a plaudit from the gods enthroned
Round the empyreum of Jove himself,
High seated on Olympus' airy top.
Nay, that his feverous voice was known to sooth
The shrill-toned prating of the females' tongues,
Who, in obedience to the lifeless song,
All prostrate fell; all, fainting, died away
In silent ecstasies of passing joy.

Ye, who oft wander by the silver light
Of sister Luna, or to church-yard's gloom,
Or cypress shades, if Chance should guide your steps
To this sad mansion, think not that you tread
Unconsecrated paths; for on this ground
Have holy streams been poured, and flowerets strewed;
While many a kingly diadem, I ween,
Lies useless here entombed, with heaps of coin
Stamped in theatric mint; — offenceless gold!
That carried not persuasion in its hue,
To tutor mankind in their evil ways.
After a lengthened series of years,
When the unhallowed spade shall discompose
This mass of earth, then relics shall be found,
Which, or for gems of worth, or Roman coins,
Well may obtrude on antiquary's eye.
Ye spouting blades! regard this ruined fane,
And nightly come within those naked walls,
To shed the tragic tear. Full many a drop
Of precious inspiration have you sucked
From its dramatic sources. Oh! look here,
Upon this roofless and forsaken pile,
And stalk in pensive sorrow o'er the ground
Where you've beheld so many noble scenes.

Thus when the mariner to foreign clime
His bark conveys, where odoriferous gales,
And orange groves, and love-inspiring wine,
Have oft repaid his toil; if earthquake dire,
With hollow groanings and convulsive pangs,
The ground hath rent, and all those beauties foiled;
Will he refrain to shed the grateful drop;
A tribute justly due (tho' seldom paid)
To the blest memory of happier times?

Robert Fergusson (1750-1774)

# *War*

*It is doubly appropriate to begin with part of Barbour's description of the battle of Bannockburn, for his poem <u>The Bruce</u> is the first-known major work in Scottish literature — it was written some ten years before Chaucer properly embarked on his Canterbury Tales —, and as a celebration of national heroism and patriotism it has few parallels in any literature. It is also history in that the events it describes took place only about sixty years before. The ballad of the <u>Battle of Otterbourne</u> celebrates another victory over the English, in 1388, as the result of a cattle raid over the Border led by the Earl of Douglas. Lord Percy is Sir Henry Percy, Shakespeare's Hotspur, and "a dead man" did win the fight in that the Scots fought on and took Percy and hundreds of his men prisoner without knowing that their leader had been dead for some hours.*

*If Bannockburn was arguably Scotland's finest hour, then the battle of Flodden was a nadir. One effect of that disaster is crystallised in Jean Elliot's song, though it was James IV's tactics as much as English "guile" that "wan the day" for England in a battle which James need not have fought. Iain Lom was poet laureate to Charles II, and related to a chief of the Macdonalds. The battle of Inverlochy in 1645 had brought against each other Montrose's Royalist army and that of the Marquis of Argyll, Chief of Clan Campbell. In this poem the hatred between certain clans is evident. And it is worth noting that at the time of the '45 rebellion, more Highlanders (including the Campbells) fought against Bonnie Prince Charlie than for him. With <u>The Hundred Pipers</u> we have now reached that campaign, and this typical Jacobite song is included also for those who know some of the words but had never realised who wrote them. <u>Johnnie Cope</u> celebrates Charles Edwards's famous victory at Prestonpans over General Sir John Cope. The battle was over in ten minutes, and the story goes that when Cope arrived on horseback at Berwick, he was congratulated on being the first general to bring the news of his "ain defeat".*

*If the plaintive note of <u>My Love's in Germany</u> strikes more keenly to the heart than the similar but more romantic sentiments expressed by Burns* *and Ann Grant, this may well be because Thomas Traill was himself a professional soldier, and he wrote the poem for his wife May, when he went to join the forces of Gustavus Adolphus in Germany in about 1630. The reality and the horror of war are caught in Bonnie George Campbell, while Burns's few lines On Thanksgiving ... will be for many as topical today in the aftermath of the Falklands campaign as ever.*

# *From* The Bruce

The Inglis archeris schot sa fast,
That mycht thair schot haff ony last,
It had bene hard to Scottis men.
Bot king Robert, that wele gan ken
That thair archeris war peralouss,
And thair schot rycht hard and grewouss,
Ordanyt, forouth the assemblé,
Hys marschell with a gret menye,                 *troop*
Fyve hundre armyt in to stele,
That on lycht horss war horsyt welle,
For to pryk amang the archeris;                  *charge*
And swa assaile thaim with thair speris,
That thai na layser haiff to schute.             *leisure*
This marschell that Ik of mute,                  *I tell of*
That Schyr Robert of Keyth was cauld,
As Ik befor her has yow tauld,
Quhen he saw the bataillis sua
Assembill, and to gidder ga,
And saw the archeris schoyt stoutly;
With all thaim off his cumpany,
In hy apon thaim gan he rid;
And our tuk thaim at a sid;
And ruschyt amang thaim sa rudly,
Stekand thaim sa dispitously,
And in sic fusoun berand doun,
And slayand thaim, for owtyn ransoun;
That thai thaim scalyt euirilkane.               *scattered every one*
And fra that tyme furth thar wes nane
That assemblyt schot to ma.                       *make*
Quhen Scottis archeris saw that thai sua
War rebutyt, thai woux hardy,
And with all thair mycht schot egrely
Amang the horss men, that thar raid;
And woundis wid to thaim thai maid;
And slew of thaim a full gret dele.
Thai bar thaim hardely and wele.
For fra thair fayis archeris war                 *enemies*

Scalyt, as I said till yow ar,
That ma na thai war be gret thing,
Swa that thai dred nocht thair schoting,
Thai woux sa hardy, that thaim thoucht
Thai suld set all thair fayis at nocht.

John Barbour (c1315-1396)

# Battle of Otterbourne

It fell about the Lammas tide
   When the muir-men win their hay,
The doughty Douglas bound him to ride
   Into England, to drive a prey.

He chose the Gordons and the Graemes,
   With them the Lindsays light and gay;
But the Jardines wald not with him ride
   And they rue it to this day.

And he has burn'd the dales of Tyne
   And part of Bambrough shire;
And three good towers on Reidswire fells,
   He left them all on fire.

And he march'd up to Newcastle
   And rode it round about:
O wha 's the lord of this castle,
   Or wha 's the lady o 't?

But up spake proud Lord Percy then,
   And O but he spake hie:
I am the lord of this castle,
   My wife's the lady gay.

If thou 'rt the lord of this castle
    Sae weel it pleases me;
For ere I cross the Border fells
    The tane of us shall die.

He took a lang spear in his hand,
    Shod with the metal free,
And for to meet the Douglas there
    He rode right furiouslie.

But O how pale his lady look'd
    Frae aff the castle wa',
When down before the Scottish spear
    She saw proud Percy fa'.

Had we twa been upon the green,
    And never an eye to see,
I wad hae had you, flesh and fell;
    But your sword sall gae wi' me.

But gae ye up to Otterbourne
    And wait there dayis three,
And if I come not ere three dayis end
    A fause knight ca' ye me.

The Otterbourne 's a bonnie burn,
    'Tis pleasant there to be;
But there is nought at Otterbourne
    To feed my men and me.

The deer rins wild on hill and dale,
    The birds fly wild from tree to tree,
But there is neither bread nor kale
    To fend my men and me.

Yet I will stay at Otterbourne
    Where you shall welcome be,
And if ye come not at three dayis end
    A fause lord I'll ca' thee.

Thither will I come, proud Percy said,
    By the might of our Ladie:
There will I bide thee, said the Douglas,
    My troth I plight to thee.

They lighted high on Otterbourne
    Upon the bent sae brown;
They lighted high on Otterbourne
    And threw their pallions down.

And he that had a bonnie boy
    Sent out his horse to grass;
And he that had not a bonnie boy,
    His ain servant he was.

But up then spake a little page
    Before the peep of dawn:
O waken ye, waken ye, my good lord,
    For Percy's hard at hand.

Ye lie, ye lie, ye liar loud,
    Sae loud I hear ye lie;
For Percy had not men yestreen
    To dight my men and me.

But I have dream'd a dreary dream
    Beyond the Isle of Sky;
I saw a dead man win a fight,
    And I think that man was I.

He belted on his guid braid sword
    And to the field he ran;
But he forgot the helmet good
    That should have kept his brain.

When Percy wi' the Douglas met
    I wat he was fu' fain:
They swakked their swords till sair they swat,
    And the blood ran down like rain.

But Percy with his good broad sword
    That could so sharply wound
Has wounded Douglas on the brow
    Till he fell to the ground.

Then he call'd on his little foot-page
    And said, Run speedilie,
And fetch my ain dear sister's son
    Sir Hugh Montgomery.

My nephew good, the Douglas said,
    What recks the death of ane;
Last night I dream'd a dreary dream
    And I ken the day's thy ain.

My wound is deep, I fain would sleep;
    Take thou the vanguard of the three,
And hide me by the braken bush
    That grows on yonder lilye lee.

O bury me by the braken bush,
    Beneath the blooming brier;
Let never living mortal ken
    That ere a kindly Scot lies here.

He lifted up that noble lord
    Wi' the saut tear in his e'e;
He hid him in the braken bush
    That his merrie men might not see.

The moon was clear, the day drew near,
    The spears in flinders flew,
But mony a gallant Englishman
    Ere day the Scotsmen slew.

The Gordons good, in English blood
    They steep'd their hose and shoon;
The Lindsays flew like fire about
    Till all the fray was done.

The Percy and Montgomery met
    That either of other were fain;
They swapped swords, and they twa swat,
    And aye the blood ran down between.

Now yield thee, yield the, Percy, he said,
    Or else I vow I'll lay thee low:
To whom must I yield, quoth Earl Percy,
    Now that I see it must be so?

Thou shalt not yield to lord nor loun
    Nor shalt thou yield to me;
But yield thee to the braken bush
    That grows upon yon lilye lee.

I will not yield to a braken bush
    Nor yet will I yield to a brier;
But I would yield to Earl Douglas,
    Or Sir Hugh the Montgomery, if he were here.

As soon as he knew it was Montgomery
    He struck his sword's point in the gronde;
The Montgomery was a courteous knight
    And quickly took him by the honde.

This deed was done at the Otterbourne
    About the breaking of the day;
Earl Douglas was buried at the braken bush
    And the Percy led captive away.

# ■ The Flowers of the Forest

I've heard them lilting at our yowe-milking —
    Lasses a-lilting before dawn of day;
But now they are moaning on ilka green loaning —
    The Flowers of the Forest are a' wede away.

At buchts, in the morning, nae blythe lads are scorning;
    Lasses are lonely and dowie and wae; —
Nae daffin', nae gabbin' — but sighing and sabbing,
    Ilk ane lifts her leglin and hies her away.

In hairst, at the shearing, nae youths now are jeering —
    Bandsters are runkled and lyart or grey:
At fair or at preaching, nae wooing, nae fleeching —
    The Flowers of the Forest are a' wede away.

At e'en in the gloaming, nae swankies are roaming,
    'Bout stacks with the lasses at bogle to play;
But ilk maid sits drearie, lamenting her dearie —
    The Flowers of the Forest are a' wede away.

Dool and wae for the order sent our lads to the Border!
    The English, for ance, by guile wan the day; —
The Flowers of the Forest, that foucht aye the foremost —
    The prime of our land — are cauld in the clay.

We'll hear nae mair lilting at the yowe-milking;
    Women and bairns are heartless and wae,
Sighing and moaning on ilka green loaning —
    The Flowers of the Forest are a' wede away.

Jean Elliot (1727-1805)

# The Day of Inverlochy

Did you hear from Cille-Cummin
How the tide of war came pouring?
Far and wide the summons travelled,
How they drave the Whigs before them!

From the castle tower I viewed it,
High on Sunday morning early,
Looked and saw the ordered battle
Where Clan Donald triumphed rarely.

Up the green slope of Cuil-Eachaidh,
Came Clan Donald marching stoutly;
Churls who laid my home in ashes,
Now shall pay the fine devoutly!

Though the earldom has been groaning
Seven long years with toil and trouble,
All the loss to plough and harrow
They shall now repay with double!

From thy side, O Laird of Lawers,
Though thy boast was in thy claymore,
Many a youth your father's clansman,
Ne'er shall rise to greet the day more!

Many a bravely mounted rider,
With his back turned to the slaughter,
Where his boots won't keep him dry now,
Learns to swim in Nevis water.

On the wings of eager rumour,
Far and wide the tale is flying,
How the slippery knaves, the Campbells,
With their cloven skulls are lying!

O'er the frosted moor they travelled,
Stoutly, with no thought of dying,
Where now many a whey-faced lubber,
To manure the fields is lying.

From the height of Tom-na-harry,
See them crudely heaped together,
In their eyes no hint of seeing,
Stretched to rot upon the heather!

Warm your welcome was at Lochy,
With blows and buffets thickening round you,
And Clan Donald's grooved claymore,
Flashing terror to confound you!

Hot and hotter grew the struggle,
Where the trenchant blade assailed them;
Sprawled with nails on ground Clan Duine,
When the parted sinew failed them.

Many a corpse upon the heather,
Naked lay, once big with daring,
From the battle's hurly-burly,
Drifting blindly to Blarchaorainn.

And another tale I'll tell you,
Never clerk declared more truly,
How the leal and loyal people
Scared the rebel folk unruly.

John of Moydart, dark the day was,
But the sail was bright that bore thee,
When thou kept thy trysting fairly,
And the Barbreac bowed before thee!

Alastair, I praise thy voyage,
Rich in glory, rich in plunder,
Alban greeted thee with joyance,
And Strathbogie's cock knocked under.

If the ill bird dulled his splendours,
When he should have shone most brightly,
With brave birds of ampler pinion,
We can learn to bear it lightly!

Alastair, with sharp-mouthed claymore,
Thou didst vow to work their ruin;
Quick their heels to flee the castle,
Quicker thou their flight pursuing!

Had the men of Mull been with thee,
Thou hadst screwed them down more tightly,
Some who fled had choked the heather,
With their traitor trunks unsightly!

Gallant son of gallant father,
Where thou warrest, thou art winner;
Woe, Saxon, to thy crazy stomach,
When MacCholla sours thy dinner!

By the field of Goirtean-oar,
Who may take his summer ramble,
He will find it fair and fattened
By the best blood of the Campbell!

If I could, I would be weeping,
For your shame and for your sorrow,
Orphans' cry and widows' wailing,
Through the long Argyll tomorrow.

Iain Lom (c1624–c1710)
Translated from the Gaelic
by John Stuart Blackie

# The Hundred Pipers

Wi' a hundred pipers an' a', an' a',
Wi' a hundred pipers an' a', an' a';
We'll up an' gie them a blaw, a blaw,
Wi' a hundred pipers an' a', an' a'.
Oh! it's owre the Border awa', awa',
It's owre the Border awa', awa',
We'll on and we'll march to Carlisle ha',
Wi' its yetts, its castell, an' a', an' a'.

Oh! our sodger lads looked braw, looked braw,
Wi' their tartans, kilts, an' a', an' a',
Wi' their bonnets, an' feathers, an' glittering gear,
An' pibrochs sounding sweet and clear.
Will they a' return to their ain dear glen?
Will they a' return, our Hieland men?
Second-sighted Sandy looked fu' wae,
And mothers grat when they marched away.
   Wi' a hundred pipers, etc.

Oh wha is foremost o' a', o', a'?
Oh wha does follow the blaw, the blaw?
Bonnie Charlie, the king o' us a', hurra'.
Wi' his hundred pipers an' a', an' a'.
His bonnet an' feather, he's wavin' high,
His prancing steed maist seems to fly,
The nor' wind plays wi' his curly hair,
While the pipers blaw in an unco flare.
   Wi' a hundred pipers, etc.

The Esk was swollen, sae red and sae deep,
But shouther to shouther the brave lads keep;
Twa thousand swam owre to fell English ground,
An' danced themselves dry to the pibroch's sound.
Dumfounder'd, the English saw — they saw —
Dumfounder'd, they heard the blaw, the blaw;

Dumfounder'd, they a' ran awa', awa',
From the hundred pipers an' a', an' a'.
    Wi' a hundred pipers an' a', an' a',
    Wi' a hundred pipers an' a', an' a',
    We'll up and gie them a blaw, a blaw,
    Wi' a hundred pipers an' a', an' a'.

Lady Nairne (1766-1845)

# ■ Johnnie Cope

Cope sent a letter frae Dunbar:
"Charlie, meet me an ye daur,
And I'll learn you the art o' war,
    If you'll meet me in the morning."

        Hey, Johnnie Cope, are ye wauking yet?
        Or are your drums a-beating yet?
        If ye were wauking I wad wait
            To gang to the coals i' the morning.

When Charlie looked the letter upon,
He drew his sword the scabbard from:
"Come, follow me, my merry merry men,
    And we'll meet Johnnie Cope in the morning!

"Now, Johnnie, be as good's your word;
Come, let us try both fire and sword;
And dinna flee away like a frighted bird,
    That's chased frae its nest in the morning."

When Johnnie Cope he heard o' this
He thought it wadna be amiss
To ha'e a horse in readiness
    To flee awa' in the morning.

Fye now, Johnnie get up and rin;
The Highland bagpipes mak' a din;
It's best to sleep in a hale skin,
    For 'twill be a bluidy morning.

When Johnnie Cope to Dunbar came
They speered at him, "Where's a' your men?"
"The deil confound me gin I ken,
    For I left them a' i' the morning."

Now, Johnnie, troth, ye are na blate
To come wi' the news o' your ain defeat,
And leave your men in sic a strait
    Sae early in the morning.

"Oh, faith," quo' Johnnie, "I got sic flegs
Wi' their claymores and philabegs;
If I face  them again, deil break my legs!
    So I wish you a gude morning."

Adam Skirving (1719-1803)

# My Love's in Germany

Oh, my love's in Germany, send him hame, send him hame,
Oh, my love's in Germany, send him hame.
   Oh, my love's in Germany,
   Lang leagues o' land and sea
   Frae Westrey and frae me. Send him hame, send him hame.
   Oh, my love's in Germany, send him hame.

Oh, weary fa' the war, send him hame, send him hame,
That tysed my love sae far, send him hame.
   Oh, were he hame again,
   How blythe we'd be and fain,
   But he's far ayont the main, send him hame, send him hame,
   Oh, my love's in Germany, send him hame.

Oh, wad some birdie say, send him hame, send him hame,
To my sodger far away, send him hame.
   How lonely sighs his May,
   Countin' year and month and day,
   For oh! her heart is wae, send him hame, send him hame,
   Oh, my love's in Germany, send him hame.

Colonel Thomas Traill (born c1600)

# The Silver Tassie

Go, fetch to me a pint o' wine,
    And fill it in a silver tassie,
That I may drink before I go
    A service to my bonnie lassie!
The boat rocks at the pier o' Leith,
    Fu' loud the wind blaws frae the Ferry,
The ship rides by the Berwick-Law,
    And I maun leave my bonie Mary.

The trumpets sound, the banners fly,
    The glittering spears are ranked ready,
The shouts o' war are heard afar,
    The battle closes deep and bloody.
It's not the roar o' sea or shore
    Wad mak me langer wish to tarry,
Nor shouts o' war that's heard afar:
    It's leaving thee, my bonie Mary!

Robert Burns (1759-1796)

# "O Where, Tell me Where"

"O where, tell me where, is your Highland laddie gone?
O where, tell me where, is your Highland laddie gone?"
"He's gone, with streaming banners, where noble deeds
    are done;
And my sad heart will tremble till he comes safely home."

"O where, tell me where, did your Highland laddie stay?
"O where, tell me where, did your Highland laddie stay?"
"He dwelt beneath the holly trees, beside the rapid Spey;
And many a blessing followed him the day he went away."

"O what, tell me what, does your Highland laddie wear?
O what, tell me what, does your Highland laddie wear?"
"A bonnet with a lofty plume, the gallant badge of war,
And a plaid across the manly breast that yet shall wear a
    star."

"Suppose, ah! suppose, that some cruel, cruel wound
Should pierce your Highland laddie and all your hopes
    confound!"
The pipes would play a cheering march, the banners round
    him fly;
The spirit of a Highland chief would lighten in his eye.

"But I will hope to see him yet, in Scotland's bonnie
    bounds;
But I will hope to see him yet, in Scotland's bonnie
    bounds.
His native land of liberty shall nurse his glorious wounds,
While wide, through all our Highland hills his warlike
    name resounds."

Ann Grant of Laggan (1755-1838)

# Bonnie George Campbell

Hie upon Hielands and laigh upon Tay
Bonnie George Campbell rode out on a day;
He saddled, he bridled, and gallant rode he,
And hame cam his guid horse, but never cam he.

Out cam his mother dear greeting fu' sair,
And out cam his bonnie bryde riving her hair;
My meadow lies green and my corn is unshorn,
My barn is to build and my baby's unborn.

Saddled and bridled and booted rode he,
A plume in his helmet, a sword at his knee;
But toom cam his saddle all bloody to see;
Oh hame cam his guid horse, but never cam he.


# On Thanksgiving for a
# National Victory

Ye hypocrites! are these your pranks?
To murder men, and give God thanks?
Desist for shame! Proceed no further:
God won't accept your thanks for Murther.

Robert Burns (1759-1796)

# Love

The Scots are not, by reputation, among the great lovers of the world. It is supposed that native reserve, coupled with a degree of Puritan repression, robs them of that ease of expression associated with Gallic and Latin lovers of gentler climes: which may be the reason behind Edward Topham's observation in 1775: "It is generally imagined that cold has the same degree of influence over the animal, as it has over the vegetable world, but in [Scotland] they are in direct opposition; for the plants are very late and the girls extremely forward."

Certainly, the range, quality and expressive power of Scottish love poetry is astonishing. With such a choice, from Henryson and the anonymous author of "When Flora had Ourfret the Firth", through the age of the courtly lyric to the 18th-century Romantics and the incomparable Burns, there is ample material to illustrate almost every facet of this eternally fascinating subject. So we have opted for a blend of poems which demand a place by reason of popular acclaim (all the Burns pieces fall into this category, as does Auld Robin Gray, Annie Laurie — the original Douglas of Fingland version —, O Waly, Waly and the two sonnets by Alexander Montgomerie), with those for which we have a personal preference or sentiment. They are roughly arranged according to what might be termed — Love's Delights: Young Lovers: Love's Torments: Lost Loves: Unobtainable Loves.

Annie Laurie actually existed. This noted beauty was the daughter of Sir Robert Laurie of Maxwelltown, but her "rolling eye" was obviously a dominant feature, as instead she married a Mr Ferguson of Craigdarroch. Grisell Baillie wrote the piece on which her poetic reputation rests — she was in other respects one of the ablest and most heroic noblewomen of her age — while keeping house for her exiled parents and brothers and sisters, of whom there were at various times 17. The problems of a prospective husband whose "tittie" (sister) objects to the match is a perennial one but in Grisell's case this did not happen. She married her childhood sweetheart and lived not only long, but well, to judge from her household accounts' books. Drummond's beautiful _Madrigal_ also perhaps needs a single gloss — turtle means, of course, turtle-dove.

Henryson's _The Testament of Cresseid_ is one of the great tragic poems of the 15th century, strong in narrative power, and displaying qualities both of compassion and of sombre moral judgment. It is a sequel to the story told in Chaucer's "Troilus and Criseyde" which Chaucer, and after him Shakespeare, based on a tale of Boccaccio. In all other respects _The Testament of Cresseid_ is an entirely original creation. The extract here, which is a passage towards the poem's end, contains a potential frisson for those who do not know the story.

_Auld Robin Gray_ was published in 1791, but the identity of its writer was a secret for 34 years until Anne Barnard admitted her authorship to Sir Walter Scott two years before her death. Isabel Stewart was the daughter of John, Lord of Lorne, and became the first Countess of Argyll. Nine of her children survived to marry, though the eldest, Archibald, was killed at Flodden, commanding the Scottish right wing. Alexander Scott was a cleric, and also a musician, who ended up owning vast estates. His well-known poem about a broken love is unusual for a courtly lyric in that the lady in question is said to have been his wife.

# A Red, Red Rose

O my Luve's like a red, red rose
   That's newly sprung in June;
O my Luve's like the melodie
   That's sweetly play'd in tune.
As fair art thou, my bonie lass,
   So deep in luve am I;
And I will luve thee still, my dear,
   Till a' the seas gang dry.

Till a' the seas gang dry, my Dear,
   And the rocks melt wi' the sun;
O I will love thee still, my dear,
   While the sands o' life shall run.
And fare thee weel, my only Luve!
   And fare thee weel a while!
And I will come again, my Luve,
   Tho' it were ten thousand mile!

Robert Burns (1759-1796)

## To his Mistress

So suete a kis yistrene fra thee I reft,     *yesternight*
   In bouing doun thy body on the bed,
   That evin my lyfe within thy lippis I left;
   Sensyne from thee my spirits wald neuer shed;    *since then*
To folou thee it from my body fled,
   And left my corps als cold as ony kie.     *key*
   Bot vhen the danger of my death I dred,
   To seik my spreit I sent my harte to thee;
Bot it wes so inamored with thyn ee,
   With thee it myndit lykuyse to remane:    *likewise*
   So thou hes keepit captive all the thrie,
   More glaid to byde then to returne agane.
Except thy breath thare places had suppleit,
Euen in thyn armes thair doutles had I deit.

Alexander Montgomerie (c1545–c1610)

## Doun The Burn, Davie

When trees did bud, and fields were green,
   And broom bloomed fair to see,
When Mary was complete fifteen,
   And love laughed in her e'e,
Blyth Davie's blinks her heart did move
   To speak her mind thus free,
"Gang doun the burn, Davie love,
   And I shall follow thee."

Now Davie did each lad surpass
   That dwelt on this burnside.
And Mary was the bonniest lass,
   Just meet to be a bride.

Her cheeks were rosy, red and white,
  Her e'en were bonnie blue,
Her looks were like Aurora bright,
  Her lips like dropping dew.

As down the burn they took their way,
  What tender tales they said;
His cheek to hers he aft did lay
  And with her bosom played.
Till baith at length impatient grown
  To be mair fully blest,
In yonder vale they leaned them down —
  Love only saw the rest.

What passed, I guess was harmless play,
  And naething, sure, unmeet,
For ganging hame I heard him say
  They liked a walk sae sweet,
And that they aften should return
  Sic pleasure to renew.
Quoth Mary, "Love, I like the burn,
  And aye shall follow you."

Robert Crawford (1695-1732)

## *From* The Gentle Shepherd

My Peggy is a young thing,
  Just enter'd in her teens,
Fair as the day, and sweet as May,
Fair as the day, and always gay:
My Peggy is a young thing,
  And I'm not very auld,
Yet well I like to meet her at
  The wauking of the fauld.

My Peggy speaks sae sweetly,
　　Whene'er we meet alane,
I wish nae wair to lay my care,
I wish nae mair of a' that's rare,
My Peggy speaks sae sweetly,
　　To all the lave I'm cauld;
But she gars a' my spirits glow,
　　At wauking of the fauld.

My Peggy smiles sae kindly,
　　Whene'er I whisper love,
That I look down on a' the town,
That I look down upon a crown.
My Peggy smiles sae kindly,
　　It makes me blyth and bauld;
And nathing gi'es me sic delight
　　As wauking of the fauld.

My Peggy sings sae saftly,
　　When on my pipe I play,
By a' the rest it is confest,
By a' the rest that she sings best.
My Peggy sings sae saftly,
　　And in her sangs are tald,
With innocence the wale of sense,
　　At wauking of the fauld.

Allan Ramsay (1684-1758)

# The Blue-Eyed Lassie

I gaed a waefu' gate yestreen,
　　A gate I fear I'll dearly rue:
I gat my death frae twa sweet een,
　　Twa lovely een o' bonie blue!

'Twas not her golden ringlets bright,
    Her lips like roses wat wi' dew,
Her heaving bosom lily-white:
    It was her een sae bonie blue.

She talk'd, she smil'd, my heart she wyl'd,
    She charm'd my soul I wist na how;
And ay the stound, the deadly wound,
    Cam frae her een sae bonie blue.
But "spare to speak, and spare to speed" —
    She'll aiblins listen to my vow:
Should she refuse, I'll lay my dead
    To her twa een sae bonie blue.

Robert Burns (1759-1796)

## *Sonnet from* The Tarantula of Love

O cruell love, why dothe thow sore assayle
my humbled harte with torments overtorne?
quhat triumphs dost thow mereit of avayle
in thralling me who is so far forlorne?
and to quhat end is shee as yet forborne
who, cairles of thy flams, thy bowe and darte,
in her great pryde doeth all thy pouer scorne,
and dois remark my flams with frosen harte?
now through my loss I am maid more expert,
and now dois see to be bot taels and dremes
that thow hes Mars and that I ove him self subvert,
with phebus bright in his resplendant beames,
    sen that my dame, the glorye of myne eyes,
    dispyseth the, and dois disdayne my cryes.

William Fowler (1560-1612)

# To his Mistress

O Rair
Preclair
Most fair,
My chois,
Repair
My cair
And spair
My lois.                                                       *loss*
O Rois                                                         *rose*
formois,                                                       *beautiful*
That gois
vith sort of thois, In Dians rout,                             *company*
Suppois
Quhat vois
Dois clois,
As fremmit fois, My hart about.                                *strange*

Restoir
To gloir
My soir,
O Deir;
My roir,
Thairfoir
Dois schoir
Deth neir:
Ewen heir
Synceir
I beir
Vith cairfull cheir In sorrow still:                           *sorrowful face*
But peir
Maist cleir
Vpsteir                                                        *stir up*
My lyf seueir, At poynt to spill.                              *ready*

John Stewart of Baldynneis (c1539-c1606)

# O, Wert Thou in the Cauld Blast

O, wert thou in the cauld blast,
   On yonder lea, on yonder lea,
My plaidie to the angry airt,
   I'd shelter thee, I'd shelter thee.
Or did misfortune's bitter storms
   Around thee blaw, around thee blaw,
Thy bield should be my bosom,
   To share it a',  to share it a'.

Or were I in the wildest waste,
   Sae black and bare, sae black and bare,
The desert were a paradise,
   If thou wert there, if thou wert there.
Or were I monarch o' the globe,
   Wi' thee to reign, wi' thee to reign,
The brightest jewel in my crown
   Wad be my queen, wad be my queen.

Robert Burns (1759-1796)

## "The Tender Snow, of Granis Soft and Quhyt"

The tender snow, of granis soft & quhyt,
 Is nocht so sone conswmit vith phebus heit,
As is my breist, beholding my delyte,
 Pyneit vith the presence of my lady sueit.   *pained*
The surging seyis, with stormie streameis repleit,
 Tormoylit nocht the wandring shipis sa sair,
As absence dois torment my werie spreit,
 Fleitting a flocht betuixt hoip & dispair.   *afloat*
My cative corps consumis with cursed cair;
 Mistrust & dreid hes baneist esperance,   *banished*
That I am forceit to perische quhae sould mair,
 & trast the wyte upon rememberance;   *blame*
Than absence, presence, remembrance, all thre,
Torment me for hir saik eternallie.

Alexander Montgomerie (c1545-c1610)

## Annie Laurie

Maxwelltown banks are bonnie
Where early fa's the dew;
Where I and Annie Laurie
Made up the promise true;
Made up the promise true;
And never forget will I,
And for bonnie Annie Laurie
I'd lay down my head and die.

She's backet like a peacock,
She's breasted like a swan,
She's jimp about the middle,
Her waist you weel may span;
Her waist you weel may span,
And she has a rolling eye,
And for bonnie Annie Laurie
I'd lay down my head and die.

Douglas of Fingland (fl. c1680)

# On Love

Love's like a Game at Tables, where your Dy
Of mad Affection doth by Fortune fly;
Which, when you think you're surest of the same,
Proves but at best a doubtful Aftergame;
For if they find your Fancy in a Blot,
It's two to one if then they take you not:
But being Gamesters you must boldly venture,
And, when you see the Point ly open, enter:
Believe me one thing, nothing brings about
A Game half won so soon, as holding out:
And next to holding out this you shall find
There's nothing worse than entring still behind:
Yet doth not all in happy Entrance ly,
When you are on, you must throw home and hy;
If you throw low and weak, believe me then,
Do what you can, they will be Bearing Men:
And if you look not all the better on,
They will play foul, bear Two instead of One.

Sir Robert Ayton (1570-1638)

# "Werena My Heart Licht I Wad Dee"

There was ance a may, and she lo'ed na men;
See biggit her bonnie bouir doun i' yon glen;
But now she cries Dule and a well-a-day!
Come doun the green gate and come here away.

When bonnie young Johnnie cam' ower the sea
He said he saw naething sae bonnie as me;
He hecht me baith rings and monie braw things;
And werena my heart licht I wad dee.

He had a wee tittie that lo'ed na me,
Because I was twice as bonnie as she;
She raised sic a pother 'twixt him and his mother,
That werena my heart licht I wad dee.

The day it was set and the bridal to be —
The wife took a dwam and lay doun to dee;
She maned, and she graned, out o' dolour and pain,
Till he vowed that he ne'er wad see me again.

His kin was for ane o' a higher degree,
Said, what had he to do wi' the like o' me?
Albeit I was bonnie, I wasna for Johnnie:
And werena my heart licht I wad dee.

They said I had neither cow nor calf,
Nor dribbles o' drink rins through the draff,
Nor pickles o' meal rins through the mill-e'e;
And werena my heart licht I wad dee.

His tittie she was baith wily and slee,
She spied me as I cam' ower the lea,
And then she ran in and made a loud din;
Believe your ain een an ye trow na me.

His bannet stood aye fu' round on his brow —
His auld ane looked aye as weel as some's new;
But now he lets 't wear ony gate it will hing,
And casts himsel' dowie upon the corn-bing.

And now he gaes drooping about the dykes
And a' he dow do is to hund the tykes;
The live-lang nicht he ne'er steeks his e'e;
And werena my heart licht I wad dee.

Were I young for thee as I ha'e been
We should ha'e been gallopin' doun on yon green,
And linkin' it on the lily-white lea;
And wow gin I were but young for thee!

Lady Grisell Baillie (1665-1746)

# ■ Madrigal

Poor turtle! thou bemoans
The loss of thy dear love,
And I for mine send forth those smoking groans:
Unhappy widow'd dove!
While all about do sing,
I at the root, thou on the branch above,
Even weary with our moans the gaudy spring.
    Yet these our plaints we do not spend in vain,
    Sith sighing zephyrs answer us again.

William Drummond of Hawthornden (1585-1649)

# *From* The Testament of Cresseid

The lipper folk to Cresseid than can draw,      *leper*
To se the equall distributioun
Of the Almous, bot quhen the gold thay saw,
Ilk ane to uther prevelie can roun,      *whisper*
And said: "Yone Lord hes mair affectioun,
How ever it be, unto yone Lazarous
Than to us all, we knaw be his Almous."

"Quhat Lord is yone" (quod scho), "have ye na feill,      *knowledge*
Hes done to us so greit humanitie?"
"Yes" (quod a Lipper man), "I knaw him weill,
Schir Troylus it is, gentill and fre."
Quhen Cresseid understude that it was he,
Stiffer than steill, thair stert ane bitter stound      *pang*
Throwout hir hart, and fell doun to the ground.

Quhen scho ouircome, with siching sair & sad,      *sighing*
With mony cairfull cry and cald ochane;
"Now is my breist with stormie stoundis stad,
Wrappit in wo, ane wretch full will of wane."      *devoid of hope*
Than swounit scho oft or scho culd refrane,      *before*
And ever in hir swouning cryit scho thus:
"O fals Cresseid and trew Knicht Troylus.

"Thy lufe, thy lawtie, and thy gentilnes,      *faithfulness*
I countit small in my prosperitie,
Sa elevait I was in wantones,
And clam upon the fickill quheill sa hie:      *wheel (of Fortune)*
All Faith and Lufe I promissit to the,
Was in the self fickill and frivolous:
O fals Cresseid, and trew Knicht Troilus.

"For lufe, of me thou keipt gude continence,                    *chastity*
Honest and chaist in conversatioun.
Of all wemen protectour and defence
Thou was, and helpit thair opinioun.
My mynd in fleschelie foull affectioun
Was Inclynit to Lustis Lecherous:
Fy fals Cresseid, O trew Knicht Troylus.

"Lovers be war and tak gude heid about
Quhome that ye lufe, for quhome ye suffer paine.
I lat yow wit, thair is richt few thairout                      *know: around*
Quhome ye may traist to have trew lufe agane.                    *in return*
Preif quhen ye will, your labour is in vaine.                    *try*
Thairfoir, I reid, ye tak thame as ye find,                     *advise*
For thay ar sad as Widdercock in Wind,                          *firm*

"Becaus I knaw the greit unstabilnes
Brukkill as glas, into my self I say,                           *brittle*
Traisting in uther als greit unfaithfulnes:                     *as*
Als unconstant, and als untrew of fay.                          *faith*
Thocht sum be trew, I wait richt few ar thay,                   *know*
Quha findis treuth lat him his Lady ruse:                       *extol*
Nane but my self as now I will accuse."

Quhen this was said, with Paper scho sat doun,
And on this maneir maid hir Testament.
"Heir I beteiche my Corps and Carioun                           *bequeath*
With Wormis and with Taidis to be rent.                         *toads*
My Cop and Clapper and myne Ornament,                           *cup: leper's gadget for*
And all my gold the Lipper folk sall have:                          *attracting attention*
Quhen I am deid, to burie me in grave.

"This Royal Ring, set with this Rubie reid,
Quhilk Troylus in drowrie to me send,                           *love token*
To him agane I leif it quhen I am deid,
To mak my cairfull deid unto him kend:
Thus I conclude schortlie and mak ane end,
My Spreit I leif to Diane quhair scho dwellis,
To walk with hir in waist Woddis and Wellis.                    *desolate: pools*

"O Diomeid, thou hes baith Broche and Belt,
Quhilk Troylus gave me in takning                    *token*
Of his trew lufe," and with that word scho swelt.    *died*
And sone ane Lipper man tuik of the Ring,
Syne buryit hir withouttin tarying:
To Troylus furthwith the Ring he bair,
And of Cresseid the deith he can declair.            *did*

Robert Henryson (fl. c1480-c1490)


# ■ Come Under my Plaidie

"Come under my plaidie, the night's gaun to fa';
Come in frae the cauld blast, the drift, and the snaw:
Come under my plaidie, and sit down beside me,
There's room in't, dear lassie, believe me, for twa.
Come under my plaidie, and sit down beside me,
I'll hap ye frae every cauld blast that can blaw:
Oh, come under my plaidie, and sit down beside me!
There's room in't, dear lassie, believe me, for twa."

"Gae 'wa wi' your plaidie, auld Donald, gae 'wa!
I fearna the cauld blast, the drift, nor the snaw:
Gae 'wa wi' your plaidie; I'll no sit beside ye,
Ye may be my gutcher; auld Donald, gae 'wa.
I'm gaun to meet Johnnie — he's young and he's bonnie;
He's been at Meg's bridal, fu' trig and fu' braw:
Oh, nane dances sae lightly, sae gracefu', sae tightly;
His cheek's like the new rose, his brow's like the snaw."

"Dear Marion, let that flee stick fast to the wa':
Your Jock's but a gowk, and has naething ava;
The hale o' his pack he has now on his back:
He's thretty, and I am but threescore and twa.

Be frank now and kindly: I'll busk ye aye finely,
To kirk or to market there'll few gang sae braw;
A bien house to bide in, a chaise for to ride in,
And flunkies to 'tend ye as aft ye ca'."

"My father's aye tauld me, my mither an a',
Ye'd mak' a gude husband, and keep me aye braw:
It's true I lo'e Johnnie — he's gude and he's bonnie,
But, wae's me! ye ken he has naething ava.
I ha'e little tocher: you've made a good offer:
I'm now mair than twenty — my time is but sma';
Sae, gi'e me your plaidie, I'll creep in beside ye,
I thocht ye'd been aulder than threescore and twa."

She crap in ayont him, aside the stane wa',
Where Johnnie was list'ning, and heard her tell a':
The day was appointed: his proud heart it dunted,
And strack 'gainst his side as if bursting in twa.
He wandered hame weary: the night it was dreary;
And, thowless, he tint his gate 'mang the deep snaw:
The owlet was screamin'; while Johnnie cried, "Women
Wad marry Auld Nick if he'd keep them aye braw!"

Hector MacNeill (1746-1818)

# ■ Ye Banks and Braes

Ye banks and braes o' bonnie Doon,
    How can ye bloom sae fresh and fair?
How can ye chant, ye little birds,
    And I sae weary fu' o' care?
Thou'lt break my heart, thou warbling bird,
    That wantons thro' the flowering thorn:
Thou minds me o' departed joys,
    Departed never to return.

Aft hae I rov'd by bonnie Doon,
  To see the rose and woodbine twine;
And ilka bird sang o' its love,
  And fondly sae did I o' mine.
Wi' lightsome heart I pu'd a rose,
  Fu' sweet upon its thorny tree;
And my fause lover stole my rose,
  But ah! he left the thorn wi' me.

Robert Burns (1759-1796)

# O Waly, Waly

O Waly, waly up the bank,
  And waly, waly down the brae,
And waly, waly by yon burnside
  Where I and my Love wont to gae.
I lent my back against an aik,
  I thought it was a trusty tree;
But first it bow'd and syne it brak:
  Sae my true Love did lichtly me.

O waly, waly, but love is bonny
  A little time while it is new;
But when 'tis auld, it waxeth cauld
  And fades awa' like morning dew.
O wherefore should I busk my head?
  O wherefore should I kame my hair?
For my true Love has me forsook,
  And says he'll never lo'e me mair.

Now Arthur's Seat sall be my bed,
  The sheets sall ne'er be prest by me;
Saint Anton's Well sall be my drink,
  Since my true Love's forsaken me.

Mart'mas wind, when wilt thou blaw
    And shake the green leaves aff the tree?
O gentle Death, when wilt thou come?
    For my life I am wearie.

'Tis not the frost, that freezes fell,
    Nor blawing snaw's inclemencie,
'Tis not sic cauld that makes me cry,
    But my Love's heart grown cauld to me.
When we came in by Glasgow town
    We were a comely sight to see:
My Love was clad in the black velvet,
    And I myself in cramasie.

But had I wist, before I kist,
    That love had been sae ill to win,
I had lock'd my heart in a case o' gowd,
    And pin'd it wi' a siller pin.
And O! if my young babe were born,
    And set upon the nurse's knee;
And I mysel were dead and gane,
    And the green grass growing over me!

# Auld Robin Gray

When the sheep are in the fauld, and the kye's a' at hame,
And a' the world to rest are gane;
The waes o' my heart fa' in showers frae my e'e,
Unkent by my gudeman, wha sleeps sound by me.

Young Jamie lo'ed me weel, and he sought me for his bride,
But saving a crown, he had naething else beside;
To mak' the crown a pound, my Jamie gaed to sea,
And the crown and the pound, they were baith for me.

He hadna been gane a twelvemonth and a day,
When my faither brak' his arm, and the cow was stown away;
My mither she fell sick — my Jamie at the sea;
And Auld Robin Gray came a-courting me.

My faither couldna work, and my mither couldna spin;
I toil'd day and nicht, but their bread I couldna win:
Auld Rob maintain'd them baith, and wi' tears in his e'e,
Said "Jeanie, for their sakes, will ye no marry me?"

My heart it said Na, and I looked for Jamie back;
But hard blew the winds, and his ship it was a wrack;
The ship was a wrack: why didna Jamie dee?
Or why am I spared to cry, "Wae is me?"

My faither urged me sair, my mither didna speak,
But she lookit in my face till my heart was like to break;
They gied him my hand — my heart was in the sea;
And so Robin Gray he was gudeman to me.

I hadna been his wife a week but only four,
When, mournfu' as I sat on the stane at my door,
I saw my Jamie's ghaist, for I couldna think it he,
Till he said: "I'm come hame, love, to marry thee."

Oh! sair, sair did we greet, and mickle say of a';
I gied him a kiss, and bade him gang awa';
I wished that I were dead, but I'm nae like to dee:
For tho' my heart is broken, I'm young, wae's me!

I gang like a ghaist, and carena to spin;
I darena think on Jamie, for that wad be a sin;
But I'll do my best a gude wife to be,
For oh! Robin Gray he is kind to me.

Lady Anne Barnard (1750-1825)

# Secret Love

Pity one that bears love's anguish
   Yet the cause that must conceal;
Sore it be to lose a dear one,
   And a wretched state to feel.

And the love I gave in secret
   I must ever keep unknown
But unless relief comes quickly
   All my freshness will be gone.

Ah! the name of my beloved
   Ne'er to other can be told;
He put me in lasting fetters —
   Pity me a hundredfold.

Isabel Stewart (died 1510)
Translated from the Gaelic
by Nigel MacNeill

# John Anderson my Jo

John Anderson my jo, John,
  When we were first acquent,
Your locks were like the raven,
  Your bonnie brow was brent;
But now your brow is beld, John,
  Your locks are like the snow;
But blessings on your frosty pow,
  John Anderson, my jo.

John Anderson my jo, John,
  We clamb the hill thegither;
And mony a canty day, John,
  We've had wi' ane anither:
Now we maun totter down, John,
  And hand in hand we'll go,
And sleep thegither at the foot,
  John Anderson, my jo.

Robert Burns (1759-1796)

# To Love, Unloved

To luve unluvit it is ane pane,
For scho that is my soverane,
Sum wantoun man so he hes set hir
That I can get no lufe agane
Bot brekis my hairt and nocht the bettir.

Quhen that I went with that sweit may          *maid*
To dance, to sing, to sport and pley,
And oft times in my armeis plet hir,           *embraced*
I do now murne both nycht and day
And brekis my hart and nocht the bettir.

Quhair I wes wont to se hir go
Rycht trimly passand to and fro,
With cumly smylis quhen that I met hir —
And now I leif in pane and wo
And brekis my hairt and nocht the bettir.

Quhattane ane glaikit fule am I               *stupid*
To slay my self with malancoly,
Sen weill I ken I may nicht get hir,
Or quhat suld be the cause and quhy
To brek my hairt and nocht the bettir.

My hairt, sen thou may nocht hir pleis,
Adew, — as gud luf cumis as gais.
Go chus ane udir and foryet hir.
God gif him dolour and diseis
That brekis thair hairt and nocht the bettir.

Alexander Scott (c1515-1583)

# Genty Tibby and Sonsy Nelly

T*ibby* has a Store of Charms,
    Her genty Shape our Fancy warms,
How starkly can her sma' white Arms
    Fetter the Lad wha looks but at her;
Frae Ancle to her slender Waste,
    These Sweets conceal'd invite to dawt her,
Her rosie Cheek and rising Breast,
    Gar ane's Mouth gush bowt fou' o' Water.

*Nelly's* gawsy, saft and gay,
Fresh as the lucken Flowers in *May*,
Ilk ane that sees her cries *Ah hey!*
    She's bonny, O I wonder at her!
The Dimples of her Chin and Cheek,
    And Limbs sae plump invite to dawt her,
Her Lips sae sweet, and Skin sae sleek,
    Gar mony Mouths beside mine water.

Now strike my Finger in a Bore,
My Wyson with the Maiden shore,
Gin I can tell whilk I am for
    When these twa Stars appear thegether.
O Love! Why dost thou gi'e thy Fires
    Sae large? while we're oblig'd to nither
Our spacious Sauls immense Desires,
    And ay be in a hankerin Swither.

*Tibby's* Shape and Airs are fine,
And *Nelly's* Beauties are divine;
But since they canna baith be mine,
    Ye Gods give Ear to my Petition,
Provide a good Lad for the tane,
    But let it be with this Provision,
I get the other to my lane,
    In Prospect *plano* and Fruition.

Allan Ramsay (1684-1758)

# "When Flora had Ourfret the Firth"

When Flora had ourfret the firth,          *adorned: grove*
   In May of every moneth quene;
When merle and mavis singis with mirth,    *blackbird: thrush*
   Sueit melling in the schawis schene;   *joining: groves: beautiful*
   When all luvaris rejoicit bene,
And most desirous of their prey;
   I heard a lusty luvar mene:          *complain*
"I luve but I dar nocht assay.

"Strang are the panis I dayly prufe
   Bot yit with patience I sustene,
I am so fetterit with the lufe
   Onlie of my lady schene,
   Whilk for hir beauty mycht be quene;
Natour sa craftily alway                   *Nature*
   Hes done depaint that sweit serene;
Whom I luf I dar nocht assay.

"Scho is so brycht of hide and hew,
   I lufe bot hir alone, I wene;
Is non hir luf that may eschew,
   That blenkis of that dulce amene.      *glances: sweet love*
   So comely cleir are hir twa ene,
That scho ma luvaris dois effrey,          *more*
   Than evir of Greece did fair Helene;
Whom I luve I dar nocht assay."

(Early 16th century)

# On Platonic Love
## To Mistress Cicely Crofts,
## Maid of Honour

O that I were all soule that I might prove
    For you as fitt a love
As you are for an Angell, for I vow,
None but pure spiritts are fitt loves for you.

You'r all Etheri'all, there is in you noe dross
    Nor any part that's gross,
Your coursest part is like the curious lawne
O're Vestall Relicts for a covering drawne.

Your other part, part of the purest fire
    That e're Heaven did inspire,
Makes every thought that is refined by it
A Quintessence of goodnes and of witt.

Thus doe your raptures reach to that degree
    In loves Phylosiphy
That you can figure to your selfe a fyre,
Void of all heate, a love without desire.

Nor in divinity doe you goe less,
    You thinke and yow profess
That soules may have a plenitude of joy,
Although there bodyes never meete t'Enjoy.

But I must needes confess I doe not finde
    The motions of my minde
Soe purifyed as yet, but at there best
My body claims in them some interest.

I hold a perfyt Ioy makes all our parts
    As joyfull as our hearts,
My senses tell me if I please not them
My love is butt a dottage or a dreame.

How shall wee then agree? you may descend,
    But will not to my end.
I faine would tune my fancy to your key,
But cannot reach to that abstracted way.

There rests but this, that, while wee sojourne here,
    Our Bodyes may draw nere,
And when our joyes they can noe more Extend,
Then lett our soules beginn where they did end.

Sir Robert Ayton (1570-1638)

# Blythe was She

*Blythe, blythe and merry was she,*
*Blythe was she butt and ben,*
*Blythe by the banks of Earn,*
*And blythe in Glenturit glen!*

By Oughtertyre grows the aik,
 On Yarrow banks the birken shaw;
But Phemie was a bonier lass
 Than braes o' Yarrow ever saw.

Her looks were like a flow'r in May,
 Her smile was like a simmer morn.
She tripped by the banks o' Earn
 As light's a bird upon a thorn.

Her bonie face it was as meek
 As onie lamb upon a lea.
The evening sun was ne'er sae sweet
 As was the blink o' Phemie's e'e.

The Highland hills I've wander'd wide,
 As o'er the Lawlands I hae been,
But Phemie was the blythest lass
 That ever trod the dewy green.

Robert Burns (1759-1796)

# *Religion*

It has often been pointed out that Scottish literature lacks anything comparable to the great mystical religious writings which are one of the glories of English literature. Perhaps a very different national temperament provides part of the explanation; certainly, for centuries a totally different kind of development in Church doctrine and discipline was inimical to the flowering of religious art of any kind.

Nonetheless, Scotland's religion has long regulated the heartbeat of Scottish life, and deeply-held beliefs will find expression. It is interesting to note that there is a far larger body of literature of all periods, directly or indirectly concerned with the spiritual side of man's experience, than of any other art in Scotland. The reason for this is not far to seek: painting, sculpture, tapestry-weaving on a grand scale, the creation of stained glass, all require patronage, and the Church, until recently, declined to patronise. Moreover, so thoroughly did the Reforming zealots of the 16th century perform their works of destruction, that very little from an earlier period remains. Writing, on the other hand, is an intimate and personal art. One notes, too, the elements of public and private conflict which characterise some of the pieces here: religion has never been a peaceful facet of Scottish life. Indeed, from before the Reformation — the period of Sir David Lyndsay and William Dunbar — the Scots seem to have found their religious expression more in disputation than in any sort of quietism.

We have tried to represent both the pre-Reformation Catholic tradition and the post-Reformation Presbyterian one. From the former come, for instance, Dunbar's <u>Rorate Celi Desuper</u>, the triumphant Christmas song <u>In Dulci Jubilo</u> and the grave little poem <u>Think on God</u>. While the Calvinistic ethos which came to pervade Scottish life in the 16th and 17th centuries is reflected in the metrical psalms — some, unchosen, famous for their incredible and sometimes hilarious verbal convolutions, but at their best a moving statement of a people's faith — and Burns' cry to his God.

# A Song of the Birth of Christ

I come from heuin to tell
The best nowellis that euer befell,
To zow thir tythingis trew I bring,
And I will of them say and sing.

This day, to zow, is borne ane childe
Of Marie meik, and Virgin milde.
That blissit bairne bening and kynde,
Sall zow reioyis, baith hart and mynde.

It is the Lord, Christ, God and Man,
He will do for zow quhat he can:
Him self zour Sauiour will be,
Fra sin and hell, to mak zow fre.

He is zour rycht Saluatioun,
From euerlasting Dampnatioun:
That ze may Ring in gloir and blis,  *reign*
For euer mair in heuin with his.

Ze sall him find, but mark or wying,  *blemish*
Full sempil in ane Cribe lying:
Sa lyis he quhilk zow hes wrocht,
And all this warld maid of nocht.

Lat vs reioyis and be blyith,
And with the Hyrdis go full swyith,  *shepherds: quickly*
And se quhat God of his grace hes done,
Throw Christ to bring vs to his throne.

My Saull and lyfe stand up and se
Quha lyis in ane Cribbe of tre;
Quhat Babe is that, sa gude and fair?
It is Christ, Goddis Sone and air.

Welcome now, gracious God of mycht,
To sinnaris vyle, pure and vnrycht. *poor*
Thow come to saif vs from distres,
How can we thank thy gentilnes!

O God that maid all Creature,
How art thow now becumit sa pure,
That on the hay and stray will ly,
Amang the Assis, Oxin and Ky?

And war the warld ten tymes sa wyde,
Cled ouer with gold, and stanis of pryde,
Unworthie it war, zit to the,
Under thy feit ane stule to be.

The Sylk and Sandell the to eis,
Ar hay, and sempill sweiling clais,
Quharin thow gloris greitist King,
As thow in heuin war in thy Ring. *Kingdom*

Thow tuke sic panis temporall,
To mak me ryche perpetuall.
For all this warldis welth and gude,
Can na thing ryche thy celsitude.

O my deir hart, zung Jesus sweit,
Prepair thy credill in my Spreit,
And I sall rock the in my hart,
And neuer mair fra the depart.

Bot I sall pryse the euer moir,
With sangis sweit vnto thy gloir:
The kneis of my hart sall I bow,
And sing that rycht Balulalow.

Gloir be to God Eternallie,
Quhilk gaif his onlie Sone for me:
The angellis Joyis for to heir,
The gracious gift of this new Zeir.

From The Gude and Godlie Ballads (1567)

# Of Christ's Nativity

*Rorate celi desuper.*
Hevins distill your balmy schouris,
For now is rissin the bricht day ster
Fro the ros Mary, flour of flouris;
The cleir sone quhome no clud devouris,
Surmunting Phebus in the est,
Is cummin of his hevinly touris
*Et nobis Puer natus est.*

Archangellis, angellis, and dompnationis,    *dominations*
Tronis, potestatis, and marteiris seir,    *many*
And all ye hevinly operationis,
Ster, planeit, firmament, and speir,    *sphere*
Fyre, erd, air, and watter cleir,
To him gife loving, most and lest,
That come in to so meik maneir
*Et nobis Puer natus est.*

Synnaris, be glaid and pennance do
And thank your makar hairtfully,
For he that ye mycht nocht cum to
To yow is cummin full humly;
Your saulis with his blud to by
And lous yow of the feindis arrest,
And only of his awin mercy
*Pro nobis Puer natus est.*

All clergy do to him inclyne
And bow unto that barne benyng,
And do your observance devyne
To him that is of kingis king;
Ensence his altar, reid and sing
In haly kirk, with mynd degest,               *composed*
Him honouring attour all thing
*Qui nobis Puer natus est.*

Celestiall fowlis in the are,
Sing with your nottis upoun hicht,
In firthis and in forrestis fair               *groves*
Be myrthfull now, at all your mycht;
For passit is your dully nycht,
Aurora hes the cluddis perst,
The son is rissin with glaidsum lycht,
*Et nobis Puer natus est.*

Now spring up, flouris, fra the rute,
Revert yow upwart naturaly,
In honour of the blissit frute
That rais up fro the rose Mary;
Lay out your levis lustely,
Fro deid tak lyfe now at the lest
In wirschip of that Prince wirthy
*Qui nobis Puer natus est.*

Syng hevin imperiall most of hicht,
Regions of air mak armony;
All fishe in flud and foull of flicht
Be myrthfull and mak melody;
All *Gloria in excelsis* cry,
Hevin, erd, se, man, bird, and best:
He that is crownit abone the sky
*Pro nobis Puer natus est.*

William Dunbar (c1460-c1521)

# In Dulci Jubilo

In dulci jubilo, now let us sing with mirth and jo,
Our hartis consolatioun lyis in praesepio;
And schynis as the Sone, Matris in gremio.
Alpha es et O, Alpha es et O.

O Jesu parvule, I thrist sore efter the:
Confort my hart and mynde, O Puer optime!
God of all grace sa kynde, et Princeps gloriae,
Trahe me post te; Trahe me post te.

Ubi sunt gaudia, in ony place, bot thair
Quhair that the angellis sing, Nova Cantica,
Bot and the bellis ring, in Regis curia.
God gif I war thair: God gif I war thair!

# Of Christ's Resurrection

Done is a battell on the dragon blak,
Our campioun Chryst confountet hes his force;
The yettis of hell ar brokin with a crak,
The signe triumphall rasit is of the croce,
The divillis trymmillis with hiddous voce,             *tremble*
The saulis ar borrowit and to the blis can go,         *redeemed*
Chryst with his blud our ransonis dois indoce:         *endorse*
*Surrexit dominus de sepulchro.*

Dungin is the deidly dragon Lucifer,                    *overcome*
The crewall serpent with the mortall stang,
The auld kene tegir with his teith on char             *bared*
Quhilk in a wait hes lyne for us so lang,
Thinking to grip us in his clowis strang:
The mercifull lord wald nocht that it wer so,
He maid him for to felye of that fang:                 *fail: prey*
*Surrexit dominus de sepulchro.*

He for our saik that sufferit to be slane
And lyk a lamb in sacrifice wes dicht,                 *prepared*
Is lyk a lyone rissin up agane,
And as a gyane raxit him on hicht:                     *giant*
Sprungin is Aurora radius and bricht,
On loft is gone the glorius Appollo,
The blisfull day depairtit fro the nycht:
*Surrexit dominus de sepulchro.*

The grit victour agane is rissin on hicht
That for our querrell to the deth wes woundit;         *sake*
The sone that wox all paill now schynis bricht,
And, dirknes clerit, our fayth is now refoundit:
The knell of mercy fra the hevin is soundit,
The Cristin ar deliverit of thair wo,
The Jowis and thair errour ar confoundit:
*Surrexit dominus de sepulchro.*

The fo is chasit, the battell is done ceis,
The presone brokin, the jevellouris fleit and flemit,  *jailers: banished*
The weir is gon, confermit is the peis,
The fetteris lowsit and the dungeoun temit,            *empty*
The ransoun maid, the presoneris redemit,
The feild is win, ourcummin is the fo,
Dispulit of the tresur that he yemit:                  *kept*
*Surrexit dominus de sepulchro.*

William Dunbar (c1460–c1521)

# Psalm 23
## (Metrical Version)

The Lord's my shepherd, I'll not want.
    He makes me down to lie
In pastures green: he leadeth me
    the quiet waters by.

My soul he doth restore again;
    and me to walk doth make
Within the paths of righteousness,
    ev'n for his own name's sake.

Yea, though I walk in death's dark vale,
    yet will I fear none ill:
For thou art with me; and thy rod
    and staff me comfort still.

My table thou hast furnished
    in presence of my foes;
My head thou dost with oil anoint,
    and my cup overflows.

Goodness and mercy all my life
    shall surely follow me:
And in God's house for evermore
    my dwelling-place shall be.

Psalter (1650)

# Psalm 124
## (Metrical Version)

Now Israel may say, and that truly,
If that the Lord had not our cause maintain'd;
If that the Lord had not our right sustain'd,
When cruel men against us furiously
Rose up in wrath to make of us their prey;

Then certainly they had devour'd us all,
And swallow'd quick, for ought that we could deem;
Such was their rage, as we might well esteem.
And as fierce floods before them all things drown,
So had they brought our soul to death quite down.

The raging streams with their proud swelling waves,
Had then our soul o'er whelmed in the deep.
But bless'd be God, who doth us safely keep,
And hath not giv'n us for a living prey
Unto their teeth, and bloody cruelty.

Ev'n as a bird out of the fowler's snare
Escapes away, so is our soul set free:
Broke are their nets, and thus escaped we.
Therefore our help is in the Lord's great name,
Who heav'n and earth by His great pow'r did frame.

Psalter (1650)

# Psalm 130

Deep sunk in floods of grief,
   Unto the Lord I prayed
That he would send relief,
   And thus my sad heart said:

Lord, hear the sighs and groans
   That I before Thee pour,
Listen unto my moans
   And help me at this hour.

If, like a judge severe,
   To punish Thou be bent,
No flesh can be so clear
   As to prove innocent.

But merciful Thou art,
   And from all passion free;
But, Lord, it is our part
   With fear to trust in Thee.

Thy word, mine only hope,
   Sustains my wavering mind,
And in that faithful prop
   All confidence I find.

No watchman of the night
   More longeth for the day
Than I do for the light
   Which Thy grace doth display.

Then trust the Lord all ye
   That do Him fear and know,
For it is only He
   That helps the weak and low.

Robert Ker, Earl of Ancrum (1578-1654)

# Think on God

Think on god that the bocht
Lang in sin ly nocht
In thy kin pryd the nocht
ffor tynt thing Cair nocht
puyr folk oppres nocht
ffor all this warld sall turne to nocht

From the Maitland Folio (16th century)

# Prayer

I praise Thee, Christ, that on Thy breast
A guilty one like me may rest;
And that Thy favour I can share;
And on my lips Thy cross may bear.

O Jesus, sanctify my heart,
My hands and feet and every part;
Me sanctify in Thy good grace, —
Blood, flesh and bones, and all my ways.

I never cease committing sin;
For still its love resides within:
May God His holy fragrance shed
Upon my heart and on my head.

Great glorious One vouchsafe relief
From all the ills that bring me grief;
Ere I am laid beneath the sod:
Before me smooth my way to God.

Muireadhach Albannach (c1180-c1220)
Translated from the Gaelic
by Nigel MacNeill

# "My Lufe Murnis for Me"

My lufe murnis for me, for me
My lufe that murnis for me,
I am not kynde, hes not in mynde
My lufe that murnis for me.

Quha is my lufe, bot God abufe,
Quhilk all this world hes wrocht;
The King of blis, my lufe he is,
Full deir he hes me bocht.

His precious blude he sched on rude,
That was to mak us fre;
This sall I preve, be Goddis leve,
That sare my lufe murnis for me.

This my lufe come fra abufe,
And borne was of ane maid:
For till fulfill, his Fatheris will,
Till filfurth that he said.                    *carry out*

Man haif in mynde, and thow be kynde,
Thy lufe that murnis for the,
How he on Rude did sched his blude,
From Sathan to mak the fre.

From The Gude and Godlie Ballads (1567)

203

# A Prayer under the Pressure of Violent Anguish

O Thou great Being! what Thou art
    Surpasses me to know:
Yet sure I am, that known to Thee
    Are all Thy works below.

Thy creature here before Thee stands,
    All wretched and distrest;
Yet sure those ills that wring my soul
    Obey Thy high behest.

Sure Thou, Almighty, canst not act
    From cruelty or wrath!
O free my weary eyes from tears,
    Or close them fast in death!

But if I must afflicted be,
    To suit some wise design;
Then man my soul with firm resolves
    To bear and not repine!

Robert Burns (1759-1796)

# A Prayer against the Plague

O eterne God of power infinyt,
To quhois hie knawlege nathing is obscure —
That is, or was, or sal be, is perfyt
Into Thy sicht quhill that this warld indure —
Haif mercy of us, indigent and peure!                        *poor*
Thow dois na wrang to puneis our offens;
O Lord, that is to mankynd haill succure,
Preserve us fra this perrelus pestilens!

We The beseik, O Lord of lordis all,
Thy eiris inclyne and heir our grit regrait!                 *lament*
We ask remeid of The in generall,
That is of help and confort desolait;
Bot Thow with rewth our hairtis recreat,                     *compassion*
We are bot deid but only Thy clemens:
We The exhort on kneis law prostrait,                        *low*
Preserf us fra this perrellus pestilens!

We ar richt glaid Thow puneis our trespass
Be ony kynd of uthir tribulatioun,
Wer it Thy will, O Lord of hevin! Allais
That we sowld thus be haistely put doun,
And dye as beistis without confessioun,
That nane dar mak with uthir residence!                      *go and stay with another*
O blissit Jesu that woir the thorny croun,
Preserve us frome this perrellus pestilens!

Use derth, O Lord, or seiknes and hungir soir,
And slaik Thy plaig that is so penetryve!                     *assuage*
Thy pepill ar perreist: quha ma remeid thairfoir,
Bot Thow, O Lord, that for thame lost Thy lyve?
Suppois our syn be to The pungityve,                         *vexatious*
Oure deid ma nathing our synnys recompens.
Haif mercy Lord: we ma not with The stryve:
Preserve us frome this perrellus pestilens!

Haif mercy Lord! Haif mercy hevynis King!
Haif mercy of Thy pepill penetent!
Haif mercy of our petous punissing!
Retreit the sentence of Thy just jugement            *withdraw*
Aganis us synnaris that servis to be schent!         *destroyed*
Without mercy we ma mak no defens:
Thow that but rewth upoun the Rude was rent
Preserve us frome this perrellus pestilens!

Remmember Lord, how deir Thow hes us bocht,          *redeemed*
That for us synnaris sched Thy pretius blude,
Now to redeme that Thow hes maid of nocht,
That is of vertew barrane and denude;
Haif rewth Lord, of Thyne awin symilitude!           *likeness*
Puneis with pety and nocht with violens!
We knaw it is for our ingratitude
That we ar puneist with this pestilens.

Thow grant us grace for till amend our miss
And till evaid this crewall suddane deid;
We knaw our syn is all the cause of this;
For oppin syn thair is set no remeid;                *obvious*
The justice of God mon puneis that bot dreid,
For by the law He will with non dispens;             *ordinances of God*
Quhair justice laikis, thair is eternall feid        *wrath*
Of God that sowld preserf fra pestilens.

Bot wald the heiddismen that sowld keip the law
Pueneis the peple for thair trangressioun,
Thair wald na deid the peple than overthraw;         *death*
Bot thay ar gevin so planely till oppressioun
That God will nocht heir thair intercessioun;
Bot all ar puneist for thair inobediens
Be sword or deid, withowttin remissioun,
And hes just cause to send us pestilens.

Superne Lucerne, guberne this pestilens; *High: control*
Preserve and serve that we not sterve thairin!
Declyne that pyne be Thy devyne prudens!
O Trewth, haif rewth — lat not our slewth us twin! *sloth: divide*
Our syt full tyt, wer we contryt, wald blin. *suffering: cease*
Dissiver did never quha-evir Thy besocht. *been abandoned*
Send grace with space, and us imbrace fra syn!
Latt nocht be tynt that Thow so deir hes bocht! *lost*

O Prince preclair, this cair cotidiane,
We The exhort, distort it in exyle!
Bot Thow remeid, this deid is bot ane trane *unless you help: strategem*
For to dissaif the laif, and thame begyle; *deceive: men*
Bot Thow sa wyis devyis to mend this byle, *outbreak*
Of this mischeif quha ma releif us ocht —
For wrangus win bot Thow our syn oursyll! *evil gain: disregard*
Lat nocht be tynt that Thow so deir hes bocht!

Sen for our vyce that justyce mon correct,
O King most hie now pacifie Thy feid! *wrath*
Our syn is huge; refuge we not suspect; *have hope of*
As Thow art juge, deluge us of this dreid: *remove from*
In tyme assent or we be schent with deid;
We us repent and tyme mispent forthocht: *regret*
Thairfoir evirmoir be gloir to Thy Godheid:
Lat nocht be tynt that Thow sa deir hes bocht!

Robert Henryson (fl. c1480-c1490)

# Rune of Hospitality

I saw a stranger yestreen;
I put food in the eating place,
Drink in the drinking place,
Music in the listening place;
In the sacred name of the Triune;
He blessed myself and my house,
My cattle and my dear ones;
And the lark said in her song,
    Often, often, often
Goes the Christ in the stranger's guise,
    Often, often, often
Goes the Christ in the stranger's guise.

Translated from the Gaelic<br>by Kenneth Macleod

# Death

*Death has exercised powerfully the imaginations of creative artists of every age and nation; it is the one inevitable aspect of the future with which all must come to terms. The reaction of the Scots in general seems to have been one which seeks relief from awesomeness in humour. Given the uncertainty of personal salvation which old-time Calvinism seems to have encouraged and the ghastly belief in eternal damnation as the alternative, it is perhaps not surprising that the Scots have often tried to make the subject bearable by laughing at it — and wisely, since there is nothing like humour to put things correctly in proportion. Humorous stories, written and unwritten, about funny funerals abound in Scotland — one of the earliest is in Tobias Smollett's Humphrey Clinker (1771). And here we have included both Burns and Fergusson wittily versifying on the subject of death.*

*It would of course be misleading to suggest that humour pervades even most of Scottish writing about death. It does not, and individual reactions vary from the sheer panic of Dunbar's "Lament for the Makaris" with its haunting Latin refrain, "The fear of death obsesses me" — perhaps the most engagingly sympathetic of all poems on death — to the cool, proud courage of Montrose, writing verse on the eve of his execution, and the comforting, pre-Calvinistic attitude of Alexander Hume's O Happie Death.*

*James Beattie was a philosopher as well as a poet. The formal, "Augustan" English style of his Epitaph, Intended for Himself is typical also of the author of a book against Scotticisms for his students at Aberdeen University, who had "no opportunity of learning English from the company they keep". As utter contrast on both counts, we have included Fergusson's Last Will. Perhaps the philosopher would have had, or had, the last laugh. The wretched Fergusson died in a madhouse when he was just 24. But above all, this section depends on the old ballads, which make their statements without conveying attitudes or trying to elicit specific reactions — wherein lies at least part of their uncanny power.*

# The Twa Corbies

As I was walking all alane,
I heard twa corbies making a mane:
The tane unto the tither did say,
"Whar sall we gang and dine the day?"

" — In behint yon auld fail dyke
I wot there lies a new-slain knight;
And naebody kens that he lies there
But his hawk, his hound and his lady fair.

"His hound is to the hunting gane,
His hawk to fetch the wild-fowl hame,
His lady's ta'en anither mate,
So we may mak' our dinner sweet.

"Ye'll sit on his white hause-bane,
And I'll pike ooot his bonny blue e'en:
Wi' ae lock o' his gowden hair
We'll theek our nest when it grows bare.

"Mony a one for him maks mane,
But nane sall ken whar he is gane:
O'er his white banes, when they are bare,
The wind sall blaw for evermair."

## "Lament for the Makaris"

I that in heill wes and gladnes
Am trublit now with gret seiknes
And feblit with infermite:
    *Timor mortis conturbat me.*

Our plesance heir is all vane glory,
This fals warld is bot transitory,
The flesche is brukle, the Fend is sle:       *devil: sly*
    *Timor mortis conturbat me.*

The stait of man dois change and vary,
Now sound, now seik, now blith, now sary,
Now dansand mery, now like to dee:
    *Timor mortis conturbat me.*

No stait in erd heir standis sickir;
As with the wynd wavis the wickir,       *branch*
Wavis this warldis vanite:
    *Timor mortis conturbat me.*

On to the ded gois all estatis,
Princis, prelotis, and potestatis,
Baith riche and pur of al degre:
    *Timor mortis conturbat me.*

He takis the knychtis in to feild,
Anarmit under helme and scheild;
Victour he is at all mellie:
    *Timor mortis conturbat me.*

That strang unmercifull tyrand
Takis, on the moderis breist sowkand,       *sucking*
The bab full of benignite:
    *Timor mortis conturbat me.*

He takis the campion in the stour,      *champion: fight*
The capitane closit in the tour,
The lady in bour full of bewte:
    *Timor mortis conturbat me.*

He sparis no lord for his piscence,      *power*
Na clerk for his intelligence;
His awfull strak may no man fle:
    *Timor mortis conturbat me.*

Art magicianis and astrologgis,
Rethoris, logicianis and theologgis,
Thame helpis no conclusionis sle:
    *Timor mortis conturbat me.*

In medicyne the most practicianis,
Lechis, surrigianis, and phisicianis,     *surgeons*
Thame self fra ded may not supple:     *deliver*
    *Timor mortis conturbat me.*

I se that makaris amang the laif     *poets: rest*
Playis heir ther pageant, syne gois to graif;
Sparit is nocht ther faculte:
    *Timor mortis conturbat me.*

He hes done petuously devour
The noble Chaucer of makaris flour,
The Monk of Bery, and Gower, all thre:
    *Timor mortis conturbat me.*

The gude Syr Hew of Eglintoun,
And eik Heryot, and Wyntoun,
He hes tane out of this cuntre:
    *Timor mortis conturbat me.*

That scorpion fell hes done infek     *infected*
Maister Johne Clerk and James Afflek
Fra ballat making and tragidie:
    *Timor mortis conturbat me.*

Holland and Barbour he hes berevit;
Allace, that he nocht with us levit
Schir Mungo Lokert of the Le:
    *Timor mortis conturbat me.*

Clerk of Tranent eik he hes tane,
That maid the Anteris of Gawane;
Schir Gilbert Hay endit hes he:        *written*
    *Timor mortis conturbat me.*

He hes Blind Hary and Sandy Traill
Slaine with his schour of mortall haill,
Quhilk Patrik Johnestoun myght nocht fle:
    *Timor mortis conturbat me.*

He hes reft Merseir his endite
That did in luf so lifly write,
So schort, so quyk, of sentence hie:
    *Timor mortis conturbat me.*

He hes tane Roull of Aberdene
And gentill Roull of Corstorphin;
Two bettir fallowis did no man se:
    *Timor mortis conturbat me.*

In Dunfermelyne he hes done roune        *talked*
With Maister Robert Henrisoun.
Schir Johne the Ros enbrast hes he:
    *Timor mortis conturbat me.*

And he hes now tane last of aw
Gud gentill Stobo and Quintyne Schaw,
Of quham all wichtis hes pete:        *pity*
    *Timor mortis conturbat me.*

Gud Maister Walter Kennedy
In poynt of dede lyis veraly;
Gret reuth it wer that so suld be:
    *Timor mortis conturbat me.*

Sen he hes all my brether tane
He will nocht lat me lif alane;
On forse I man his nyxt pray be:      *perforce*
   *Timor mortis conturbat me.*

Sen for the deid remeid is none,
Best is that we for dede dispone
Eftir our deid that lif may we:
   *Timor mortis conturbat me.*

William Dunbar (c1460—c1521)


# Written on the Eve of his Execution

Let them bestow on every airth a limb,
Then open all my veins that I may swim
To thee, my Maker, in that crimson lake;
Then place my parboiled head upon a stake,
Scatter my ashes, strew them in the air —
Lord! Since thou knowest where all these atoms are,
I'm hopeful thou'lt recover once my dust,
And confident thou'lt raise me with the just.

James Graham, Marquis of Montrose (1612—1650)

## O Happie Death

O happie death, to life the readie way,
    The end of greefe, and salve of sorrowes all;
O pleasant sleepe, thy paines they are bot play;
    Thy coup is sweete, although it taste of gall.
    Thou brings the bound and wretched out of thrall
Within the port sure from the stormie blast,
    For after death na mischiefe may befall,
But wo, wan-chance, and perrels all are past.
Of kindelie death nane suld affraied be
But sich as hope for na felicitie.

Alexander Hume (1560—1609)

## The Land o' the Leal

I'm wearin' awa', John,
Like snaw-wreaths in thaw, John;
I'm wearin' awa'
    To the land o' the leal.
There's nae sorrow there, John,
There's neither cauld nor care, John:
The day is aye fair
    In the land o' the leal.

Our bonnie bairn's there, John,
She was baith gude and fair, John;
And oh! we grudged her sair
    To the land o' the leal.
But sorrow's sel' wears past, John,
And joy's a-comin' fast, John —
The joy that's aye to last
    In the land o' the leal.

Sae dear's that joy was bought, John,
Sae free the battle fought, John,
That sinfu' man e'er brought
    To the land o' the leal.
Oh, dry your glist'ning e'e, John!
My saul langs to be free, John;
And angels beckon me
    To the land o' the leal.

Oh, haud ye leal and true, John!
Your day it's wearin' thro', John;
And I'll welcome you
    To the land o' the leal.
Now fare ye weel, my ain John,
This warld's cares are vain, John;
We'll meet, and we'll be fain
    In the land o' the leal.

Lady Nairne (1766—1845)


# Tam the Chapman

As Tam the Chapman on a day
Wi' Death forgather'd by the way,
Weel pleas'd, he greets a wight sae famous,
And Death was nae less pleased wi' Thomas,
Wha cheerfully lays down the pack,
And there blaws up a hearty crack;
His social, friendly, honest heart,
Sae tickled Death they could na part:
Sae after viewing knives and garters,
Death takes him hame to gie him quarters.

Robert Burns (1759—1796)

# Bessie Bell and Mary Gray

O Bessie Bell and Mary Gray,
    They war twa bonnie lasses;
They bigget a bower on yon burn-brae,
    And theekit it ower wi' rashes.

They theekit it ower wi' rashes green,
    They theekit it ower wi' heather;
But the pest cam frae the burrows-toun,
    And slew them baith thegither.

They thought to lie in Methven kirkyard
    Amang their noble kin,
But they maun lie in Stronach haugh
    To biek fornent the sin.

And Bessie Bell and Mary Gray
    They war twa bonnie lassies;
They bigget a bower on yon burn-brae,
    And theekit it ower wi' rashes.


# Epitaph, Intended for Himself

Escaped the gloom of mortal life, a soul
    Here leaves its mouldering tenement of clay,
Safe where no cares their whelming billows roll,
    No doubts bewilder, and no hopes betray.

Like thee, I once have stemm'd the sea of life;
    Like thee, have languish'd after empty joys;
Like thee, have labour'd in the stormy strife;
    Been grieved for trifles, and amused with toys.

Yet, for a while, 'gainst Passion's threatful blast
  Let steady Reason urge the struggling oar;
Shot through the dreary gloom, the morn at last
  Gives to thy longing eye the blissful shore.

Forget my frailties, thou art also frail;
  Forgive my lapses, for thyself mayst fall;
Nor read, unmoved, my artless tender tale,
  I was a friend, O man! to thee, to all.

James Beattie (1735—1803)

# My Last Will

While sober folks, in humble prose,
Estate, and goods, and gear, dispose,
A poet surely may disperse
His moveables in doggerel verse;
And, fearing death my blood will fast chill,
I hereby constitute my last will.

  Then, wit ye me to have made o'er
To Nature my poetic lore:
To her I give and grant the freedom
Of paying to the bards who need 'em
As many talents as she gave,
When I became the Muse's slave.

  Thanks to the gods, who made me poor!
No lukewarm friends molest my door,
Who always shew a busy care
For being legatee or heir.
Of this stamp none will ever follow
The youth that's favoured by Apollo.

But to those few who know my case,
Nor thought a poet's friend disgrace,
The following trifles I bequeath,
And leave them with my kindest breath;
Nor will I burden them with payment,
Of debts incurred, or coffin raiment,
As yet 'twas never my intent
To pass an Irish compliment.

To Jamie Rae, who oft, *jocosus,*
With me partook of cheering doses,
I leave my snuff-box to regale
His senses after drowsy meal,
And wake remembrance of a friend
Who lov'd him to his latter end:
But if this pledge should make him sorry,
And argue like *memento mori,*
He may bequeath't 'mong stubborn fellows
To all the finer feelings callous,
Who think that parting breath's a sneeze
To set sensations all at ease.

To Oliphant, my friend, I legate
Those scrolls poetic, which he may get,
With ample freedom to correct
Those writs I ne'er could retrospect;
With power to him and his succession,
To print and sell a new impression:
And here I fix on Ossian's head
A domicil for Doric reed,
With as much power *ad Musæ bona*
As I *in propria persona.*

To Hamilton I give the task
Outstanding debts to crave and ask;
And that my Muse he may not dub ill,
For loading him with so much trouble,
My debts I leave him *singulatim,*
As they are mostly *desperatim.*

To thee, whose genius can provoke
Thy passions to the bowl or sock;
For love to thee, Woods! and the Nine,
Be my immortal Shakespeare thine.
Here may you through the alleys turn,
Where Falstaff laughs, where heroes mourn,
And boldly catch the glowing fire
That dwells in raptures on his lyre.

Now, at my dirge (if dirge there be),
Due to the Muse and Poetry,
Let Hutchison attend; for none is
More fit to guide the ceremonies:
As I, in health, with him would often
This clay-built mansion wash and soften,
So let my friends with him partake
The generous wine at dirge or wake.—

And I consent to registration
Of this my will for preservation,
That patent it may be, and seen,
In Walter's Weekly Magazine.
Witness whereof, these presents wrote are
By William Blair, the public notar,
And, for the tremour of my hand,
Are signed by him at my command.

Robert Fergusson (1750—1774)

# On James Smith

Lament him, Mauchline husbands a',
    He aften did assist ye;
For had ye staid hale weeks awa',
    Your wives they ne'er had miss'd ye!

Ye Mauchline bairns, as on ye pass
    To school in bands thegither,
O, tread ye lightly on his grass, —
    Perhaps he was your father!

Robert Burns (1759—1796)


# On the Death of
# Mr Thomas Lancashire, Comedian

Alas, poor Tom! how oft, with merry heart,
Have we beheld thee play the Sexton's part?
Each comic heart must now be grieved to see
The Sexton's dreary part performed on thee.

Robert Fergusson (1750—1774)

# The Bonny Earl o' Moray

Ye Highlands and ye Lawlands,
   O where hae ye been?
They hae slain the Earl o' Moray,
   And hae laid him on the green.

Now wae be to thee, Huntley!
   And whairfore did ye sae!
I bade you bring him wi' you,
   But forbade you him to slay.

He was a braw gallant,
   And he rid at the ring;
And the bonny Earl o' Moray,
   O he might hae been a king!

He was a braw gallant,
   And he play'd at the ba';
And the bonny Earl o' Moray
   Was the flower amang them a'.

He was a braw gallant,
   And he play'd at the gluve;
And the bonny Earl o' Moray,
   O he was the Queen's luve!

O lang will his Lady
   Look owre the Castle Downe,
Ere she see the Earl o' Moray
   Come sounding through the town!

# The Lament of the Border Widow

My Love he built me a bonny bower
And clad it a' wi' lilye flour;
A brawer bower ye ne'er did see
Than my true love he built for me.

There came a man by middle day,
He spied his sport and went away,
And brought the king, that very night,
Who brake my bower and slew my knight.

He slew my knight to me sae dear,
He slew my knight and poin'd his gear;
My servants all for life did flee
And left me in extremitie.

I sew'd his sheet, making my mane,
I watched the corpse myself alane,
I watched his body night and day;
No living creature came that way.

I took his body on my back,
And whiles I gaed, and whiles I sate;
I digg'd a grave and laid him in,
And happ'd him with the sod sae green.

But think na ye my heart was sair
When I laid the moul on his yellow hair?
O think na ye my heart was wae
When I turn'd about, away to gae?

Nae living man I'll love again
Since that my lovely knight is slain;
Wi' ae lock of his yellow hair
I'll chain my heart for evermair.

# Rare Willy Drowned in Yarrow

"Willy's rare, and Willy's fair,
  And Willy's wondrous bonny;
And Willy heght to marry me,
  Gin e'er he marryd ony.

"Yestreen I made my bed fu' braid
  The night I'll make it narrow,
For a' the live-long winter's night
  I lie twin'd of my marrow.

"O came ye by yon water-side?
  Pu'd you the rose or lily?
Or came you by yon meadow green?
  Or saw you my sweet Willy?"

She sought him east, she sought him west,
  She sought him braid and narrow;
Sine, in the clifting of a craig,
  She found him drown'd in Yarrow.

# A Lyke-Wake Dirge

This ae nighte, this ae nighte,
  *Every nighte and alle,*
Fire, and sleet, and candle-lighte;
  *And Christe receive thye saule.*

When thou from hence away art paste,
  *Every nighte and alle,*
To Whinny-muir thou comest at laste;
  *And Christe receive thye saule.*

If ever thou gavest hosen and shoon,
  *Every nighte and alle,*
Sit thee down and put them on;
  *And Christe receive thye saule.*

If hosen and shoon thou ne'er gavest nane,
*Every nighte and alle,*
The whinnes sall pricke thee to the bare bane;
*And Christe receive thye saule.*

From Whinny-muir when thou mayst passe,
*Every nighte and alle,*
To Brig o' Dread thou comest at laste;
*And Christe receive thye saule.*

From Brig o' Dread when thou mayst passe
*Every nighte and alle,*
To purgatory fire thou comest at laste;
*And Christe receive thye saule.*

If ever thou gavest meate or drinke,
*Every nighte and alle,*
The fire sall never make thee shrinke:
*And Christe receive thye saule.*

If meate or drinke thou gavest nane,
*Every nighte and alle,*
The fire will burn thee to the bare bane;
*And Christe receive thye saule.*

This ae nighte, this ae nighte,
*Every nighte and alle,*
Fire, and sleet, and candle-lighte;
*And Christe receive thye saule.*

# The Supernatural

Death and the supernatural walk often hand in hand. Belief in the supernatural is as ancient as human kind, and nowhere on earth has such belief been stronger and more deep-rooted than on the fringes of northern Europe, the lands of impenetrable forests, long winter nights, and Christianity inextricably intermingled with older, darker practices. Such was Scotland. In enlightened, modern times, of course, we pride ourselves on our scepticism, and employ psychological jargon to explain away the terrors of our ancestors; few of us, however, fail to appreciate, imaginatively at least, the feelings expressed in the lines of Coleridge:

> Like one that on a lonesome road
> Doth walk in fear and dread,
> And having once turned round walks on,
> And turns no more his head;
> Because he knows, a frightful fiend
> Doth close behind him tread.

And this may partly explain our continuing enjoyment, and the success, of the ghostly in literature and on film.

The traditional manifestation of the supernatural in Scottish literature is best illustrated in the 15th and 16th-century Border ballads, but predating them probably by hundreds of years, and still transmitted orally long after the ballads had passed into literature, are the Gallic verses collected and translated by Alexander Carmichael in the second half of the 19th century. These, uniquely, occupy the debatable land between orthodoxy and superstition. While illuminated from within by a clear faith in Christ and the Saints of the Celtic calendar, they can also suggest most strongly the tension between these and the "other powers" which lurk in the hinterland of religious belief. Invocation of Christ against the power of "untoward fays" is frequent and explicit, and there are many poems and prayers concerning omens, in no early Christian context. We have represented this tradition by the piece Omens. To those that do not know them, we would recommend as a source of fresh information and delight the collected editions of these poems, *published originally under the title of "Carmina Gaedelica".*

*The old ballads are never better than when they are dealing with supernatural themes. Their detached style, economy of language and incremental repetition tend remorselessly to climaxes of horror, woe and amazement. Burns uses this form to great effect in his miniature ghost story Fine Flowers in the Valley. And for a classic, we have chosen the same poet's Tam o' Shanter. This is a tale of terror, enough, but lightened throughout by a marvellous vein of humour, a quality which one finds, rather differently deployed, two hundred years earlier in the ballad of Thomas the Rhymer. The surface of this ballad is light enough: True Thomas shares with Tam a certain jaunty courage, which may well be equated with total lack of discretion, and his determination to kiss the fairy woman and take the consequences is somehow very Scottish — as is his robust dismissal of her proffered gift of "the tongue that can never lee". But there are images of horror, and undertones of moral judgment, and we are left, despite our amusement, after reading both poems, with an uneasy awareness of the dark areas of the mind which underlie our everyday pre-occupations.*

# Sweet William's Ghost

As Lady Marg'ret sat in her bow'r,
    In her bow'r all alone,
There came a ghost to her bow'r door,
    With many a grievous groan.

"Oh, is it my father? oh, is it my mother?
    Or is it my brother John?
Or is it sweet William, my ain true love,
    To Scotland new come home?"

"It is not your father, it is not your mother,
    It is not your brother John;
But it is sweet William, your ain true love,
    To Scotland new come home."

"Ha'e ye brought me any fine things,
    Any new thing for to wear?
Or ha'e ye brought a braid of lace
    To snood up my gowden hair?"

"I've brought ye nae fine things at all,
    Nor any new thing to wear,
Nor ha'e I brought ye a braid of lace
    To snood up your gowden hair."

"But sweet Marg'ret! O dear Marg'ret!
    I pray thee, speak to me;
Give me my faith and troth, Marg'ret,
    As I gave it to thee."

"Thy faith and troth thou's never get,
    Nor will I with thee twin,
Till that thou come within my bow'r,
    And kiss me cheek and chin."

"My lips they are sae bitter," he says,
　"My breath it is sae strang;
If you get ae kiss of my clay-cauld lips,
　Your days will not be lang.

"O sweet Marg'ret! O dear Marg'ret!
　O Marg'ret of veritie,
Give me my faith and troth again,
　As I gave them to thee."

"Thy faith and troth thou's never get!
　Fast to them will I cling,
Till you take me to yonder kirk,
　And wed me with a ring."

"Do you not see my cheeks, Marg'ret,
　Sae sunken and sae wan?
Do you not see, my dear Marg'ret,
　I am nae earthly man?

"My body lies in yon kirkyard,
　Close by the rolling sea;
And it is but my ghost, Marg'ret,
　That's speaking now to thee.

"Then sweet Marg'ret! O dear Marg'ret!
　I pray thee, for charitie,
To give me back my faith and troth,
　As I gave them to thee."

"Your faith and troth ye shall not get,
　Nor will I twin with thee,
Till ye tell me of heaven's joys,
　Or hell's pains, how they be."

"The joys of heaven I wot not of,
　The pains of hell I dree;
But I hear the cocks begin to craw,
　Sae I must hence frae thee.

"The cocks are crawing, dear Marg'ret,
    The cocks are crawing again;
The dead must now part frae the quick,
    And sae I must be gane."

No more the ghost to Marg'ret said,
    But with a grievous groan
Evanished in a cloud of mist,
    And left her all alone.

Now she has kilted her robes of green
    A piece below her knee,
And all the live-lang winter night
    The dead corp follow'd she.

She follow'd high, she follow'd low,
    To yonder kirkyard lone,
And there the deep grave open'd up,
    And William he sank down.

"Oh, what three things are these, William,
    That stand here at your head?"
"Oh, it's three maidens, sweet Marg'ret,
    I promised once to wed."

"Oh, what three things are these, William,
    That stand close at your side?"
"Oh, it is three babies, Marg'ret,
    That these three maidens had."

"Oh, what three things are these, William,
    That lye close at your feet?"
"Oh, it is three hell-hounds, Marg'ret,
    Waiting my saul to keep."

Then she's ta'en up her white, white hand,
    And struck him on the breast,
"Have there again your faith and troth,
    And I wish your saul good rest."

# Tam o' Shanter

When chapman billies leave the street,
And drouthy neibors, neibors meet;
As market days are wearing late,
And folk begin to tak the gate,
While we sit bousing at the nappy,
An' getting fou and unco happy,
We think na on the lang Scots miles,
The mosses, waters, slaps and stiles,
That lie between us and our hame,
Where sits our sulky, sullen dame,
Gathering her brows like gathering storm,
Nursing her wrath to keep it warm.
　　This truth fand honest Tam o' Shanter,
As he frae Ayr ae night did canter:
(Auld Ayr, wham ne'er a town surpasses,
For honest men and bonie lasses).
　　O Tam! had'st thou but been sae wise,
As taen thy ain wife Kate's advice!
She tauld thee weel thou was a skellum,
A blethering, blustering, drunken blellum;
That frae November till October,
Ae market-day thou was na sober;
That ilka melder wi' the Miller,
Thou sat as lang as thou had siller;
That ev'ry naig was ca'd a shoe on
The Smith and thee gat roarin fou on;
That at the L—d's house, ev'n on Sunday,
Thou drank wi' Kirkton Jean till Monday,
She prophesied that late or soon,
Thou wad be found, deep drown'd in Doon,
Or catch'd wi' warlocks in the mirk,
By Alloway's auld, haunted kirk.
　　Ah, gentle dames! it gars me greet,
To think how mony counsels sweet,
How mony lengthen'd, sage advices,
The husband frae the wife despises!
　　But to our tale:— Ae market night,

Tam had got planted unco right,
Fast by an ingle, bleezing finely,
Wi reaming swats that drank divinely;
And at his elbow, Souter Johnie,
His ancient, trusty, drouthy crony:
Tam lo'ed him like a very brither;
They had been fou for weeks thegither.
The night drave on wi' sangs an' clatter;
And aye the ale was growing better:
The Landlady and Tam grew gracious,
Wi' favours secret, sweet and precious:
The Souter tauld his queerest stories;
The Landlord's laugh was ready chorus:
The storm without might rair and rustle,
Tam did na mind the storm a whistle.

Care, mad to see a man sae happy,
E'en drown'd himsel amang the nappy.
As bees flee hame wi' lades o' treasure,
The minutes wing'd their way wi' pleasure:
Kings may be blest, but Tam was glorious,
O'er a' the ills o' life victorious!

But pleasures are like poppies spread,
You seize the flow'r, its bloom is shed;
Or like the snow falls in the river,
A moment white — then melts for ever;
Or like the Borealis race,
That flit ere you can point their place;
Or like the Rainbow's lovely form
Evanishing amid the storm. —
Nae man can tether Time nor Tide,
The hour approaches Tam maun ride;
That hour, o' night's black arch the key-stane,
That dreary hour he mounts his beast in;
And sic a night he taks the road in,
As ne'er poor sinner was abroad in.

The wind blew as 'twad blawn its last;
The rattling showers rose on the blast;
The speedy gleams the darkness swallow'd;
Loud, deep, and lang the thunder bellow'd:

That night, a child might understand,
The deil had business on his hand.

   Weel-mounted on his grey mare Meg,
A better never lifted leg,
Tam skelpit on thro' dub and mire,
Despising wind, and rain, and fire;
Whiles holding fast his gude blue bonnet,
Whiles crooning o'er some auld Scots sonnet,
Whiles glow'rin round wi' prudent cares,
Lest bogles catch him unawares;
Kirk-Alloway was drawing nigh,
Where ghaists and houlets nightly cry.

   By this time he was cross the ford,
Where in the snaw the chapman smoor'd;
And past the birks and meikle stane,
Where drunken Charlie brak's neck-bane;
And thro' the whins, and by the cairn,
Where hunters fand the murder'd bairn;
And near the thorn, aboon the well,
Where Mungo's mither hang'd hersel'.
Before him Doon pours all his floods,
The doubling storm roars thro' the woods,
The lightnings flash from pole to pole,
Near and more near the thunders roll,
When, glimmering thro' the groaning trees,
Kirk-Alloway seem'd in a bleeze,
Thro' ilka bore the beams were glancing,
And loud resounded mirth and dancing.

   Inspiring bold John Barleycorn!
What dangers thou canst make us scorn!
Wi' tippenny, we fear nae evil;
Wi' usquabae, we'll face the devil!
The swats sae ream'd in Tammie's noddle,
Fair play, he car'd na deils a boddle,
But Maggie stood, right sair astonish'd,
Till, by the heel and hand admonish'd,
She ventur'd forward on the light;
And, wow! Tam saw an unco sight!

   Warlocks and witches in a dance:

Nae cotillon, brent new frae France,
But hornpipes, jigs, strathspeys, and reels,
Put life and mettle in their heels.
A winnock-bunker in the east,
There sat auld Nick, in shape o' beast;
A towzie tyke, black, grim, and large,
To gie them music was his charge:
He screw'd the pipes and gart them skirl,
Till roof and rafters a' did dirl. —
Coffins stood round, like open presses,
That shaw'd the Dead in their last dresses;
And (by some devilish cantraip sleight)
Each in its cauld hand held a light.
By which heroic Tam was able
To note upon the haly table,
A murderer's banes, in gibbet-airns;
Twa span-lang, wee, unchristened bairns;
A thief, new-cutted frae a rape,
Wi' his last gasp his gab did gape;
Five tomahawks, wi' blude red-rusted:
Five scimitars, wi' murder crusted;
A garter which a babe had strangled:
A knife, a father's throat had mangled.
Whom his ain son of life bereft,
The grey-hairs yet stack to the heft;
Wi' mair of horrible and awfu',
Which even to name wad be unlawfu'.

As Tammie glowr'd, amaz'd, and curious,
The mirth and fun grew fast and furious;
The Piper loud and louder blew,
The dancers quick and quicker flew,
They reel'd, they set, they cross'd, they cleekit,
Till ilka carlin swat and reekit,
And coost her duddies to the wark,
And linkit at it in her sark!

Now Tam, O Tam! had they been queans,
A' plump and strapping in their teens!
Their sarks, instead o' creeshie flainen,
Been snaw-white seventeen-hunder linen! —

Thir breeks o' mine, my only pair,
That ance were plush, o' guid blue hair,
I wad hae gien them off my hurdies,
For ae blink o' the bonie burdies!
But wither'd beldams, auld and droll,
Rigwoodie hags wad spean a foal,
Louping an' flinging on a crummock,
I wonder did na turn thy stomach.
    But Tam kent what was what fu' brawlie:
There was ae winsome wench and waulie
That night enlisted in the core,
Lang after ken'd on Carrick shore;
(For mony a beast to dead she shot,
And perish'd mony a bonie boat,
And shook baith meikle corn and bear,
And kept the country-side in fear);
Her cutty sark, o' Paisley harn,
That while a lassie she had worn,
In longitude tho' sorely scanty,
It was her best, and she was vauntie.
Ah! little ken'd thy reverend grannie,
That sark she coft for her wee Nannie,
Wi' twa pund Scots ('twas a' her riches),
Wad ever grac'd a dance of witches!
    But here my Muse her wing maun cour,
Sic flights are far beyond her power;
To sing how Nannie lap and flang
(A souple jade she was and strang),
And how Tam stood, like ane bewitch'd,
And thought his very een enrich'd:
Even Satan glowr'd, and fidg'd fu' fain,
And hotch'd and blew wi' might and main:
Till first ae caper, syne anither,
Tam tint his reason a' thegither,
And roars out, "Weel done, Cutty-sark!"
And in an instant all was dark:
And scarcely had he Maggie rallied,
When out the hellish legion sallied.
    As bees bizz out wi' angry fyke,

When plundering herds assail their byke;
As open pussie's mortal foes,
When, pop! she starts before their nose;
As eager runs the market-crowd,
When "Catch the thief!" resounds aloud;
So Maggie runs, the witches follow,
Wi' mony an eldritch skreich and hollow.

Ah, Tam! Ah, Tam! thou'll get thy fairin!
In hell, they'll roast thee like a herrin!
In vain thy Kate awaits thy comin!
Kate soon will be a woefu' woman!
Now, do thy speedy-utmost, Meg,
And win the key-stone o' the brig;
There, at them thou thy tail may toss,
A running stream they dare na cross.
But ere the keystane she could make,
The fient a tail she had to shake!
For Nannie, far before the rest,
Hard upon noble Maggie prest,
And flew at Tam wi' furious ettle;
But little wist she Maggie's mettle!
Ae spring brought off her master hale,
But left behind her ain grey tail:
The carlin claught her by the rump,
And left poor Maggie scarce a stump.

Now, wha this tale o' truth shall read,
Ilk man, and mother's son, take heed:
Whene'er to Drink you are inclin'd,
Or Cutty-sarks rin in your mind,
Think ye may buy the joys o'er dear;
Remember Tam o' Shanter's mare.

Robert Burns (1759—1796)

# The Earl of Mar's Daughter

It was intil a pleasant time,
 Upon a simmer's day,
The noble Earl of Mar's daughter
 Went forth to sport and play.

As thus she did amuse hersel'
 Below a green aik tree,
There she saw a sprightly doo
 Set on a tower sae hie.

"O Cow-me-doo, my love sae true,
 If ye'll come down to me,
Ye'se ha'e a cage of gude red gowd,
 Instead of simple tree:

"I'll put gowd hingers roun' your cage,
 And silver roun' your wall;
I'll gar ye shine as fair a bird
 As ony of them all."

But she had not these words well spoke,
 Nor yet these words well said,
Till Cow-me-doo flew frae the tower,
 And lighted on her head.

Then she has brought this pretty bird
 Hame to her bow'rs and hall,
And made him shine as fair a bird
 As ony of them all.

When day was gane and night was come,
 About the evening tide,
This lady spied a sprightly youth
 Stand straight up by her side.

"From whence came ye, young man?" she said,
    "That does surprise me sair;
My door was bolted right secure;
    What way ha'e ye come here?"

"Oh, haud your tongue, ye lady fair,
    Let all your folly be;
Mind ye not on your turtle doo,
    Last day ye brought with thee?"

"Oh, tell me mair, young man," she said;
    "This does surprise me now;
But what country ha'e ye come frae?
    What pedigree are you?"

"My mither lives on foreign isles;
    She has nae mair but me;
She is a queen of wealth, and state,
    And birth, and high degree.

"Likewise well skill'd in magic spells,
    As ye may plainly see;
And she transform'd me to yon shape,
    To charm such maids as thee.

"I am a doo the live-lang day,
    A sprightly youth at night;
This ayè gars me appear mair fair
    In a fair maiden's sight.

"And it was but this very day
    That I came o'er the sea;
Your lovely face did me enchant:
    I'll live and dee with thee."

"O Cow-me-doo, my luve sae true,
    Nae mair frae me ye'se gae."
"That's never my intent, my luve;
    As ye said, it shall be sae."

Then he has staid in bow'r with her
    For sax lang years and ane,
Till sax young sons to him she bare,
    And the seventh she's brought hame.

But aye as ever a child was born,
    He carried them away,
And brought them to his mither's care,
    As fast as they cou'd fly.

Thus he has staid in bow'r with her
    For twenty years and three;
Then came a lord of high renown
    To court this fair ladye.

But still his proffer she refused,
    And all his presents too;
Says — "I'm content to live alane,
    With my bird, Cow-me-doo."

Her father sware a solemn oath
    Amang the nobles all, —
"The morn, or ere I eat or drink,
    This bird I kill it shall."

The bird was sitting in his cage,
    And heard what they did say;
And when he found they were dismiss'd,
    Says — "Waes me for this day.

"Before that I do langer stay,
    And thus to be forlorn,
I'll gang unto my mither's bow'r,
    Where I was bred and born."

Then Cow-me-doo took flight and flew
    Beyond the raging sea;
And lighted near his mither's castle,
    On a tower of gowd sae hie.

As his mither was walking out,
    To see what she cou'd see,
It's there she saw her little son
    Set on the tower sae hie.

"Get dancers here to dance," she said,
    "And minstrels for to play;
For here's my young son, Florentine,
    Come here with me to stay."

"Get nae dancers to dance, mither,
    Nor minstrels for to play;
For the mither of my seven sons,
    The morn's her wedding day."

"Oh, tell me, tell me, Florentine,
    Tell me, and tell me true;
Tell me this day, without a flaw,
    What I will do for you."

"Instead of dancers to dance, mither,
    Or minstrels for to play,
Turn four-and-twenty wall-wight men,
    Like storks, in feathers gray;

"My seven sons to seven swans,
    Aboon their heads to flee;
And I, mysel', a gay gos-hawk,
    A bird of high degree."

Then sighin', said the queen hersel',
    "That thing's too high for me;"
But she applied to an auld woman,
    Who had mair skill than she.

Instead of dancers to dance a dance,
    Or minstrels for to play,
Four-and-twenty wall-wight men
    Turn'd birds of feathers gray;

Her seven sons to seven swans,
    Aboon their heads to flee;
And he, himsel', a gay gos-hawk,
    A bird of high degree.

This flock of birds took flight and flew
    Beyond the raging sea;
And landed near the Earl Mar's castle,
    Took shelter in every tree.

They were a flock of pretty birds,
    Right comely to be seen;
The people view'd them with surprise
    As they danced on the green.

These birds ascended frae the tree,
    And lighted on the hall;
And at the last with force did flee
    Amang the nobles all.

The storks there seiz'd some of the men,
    They cou'd neither fight nor flee;
The swans they bound the bride's best man
    Below a green aik tree.

They lighted next on maidens fair,
    Then on the bride's own head;
And with the twinkling of an e'e
    The bride and them were fled.

There's ancient men at weddings been,
    For sixty years or more;
But sic a curious wedding-day
    They never saw before.

# Up in the Air

Now the Sun's gane out o' Sight,
Beet the Ingle, and snuff the Light:
In Glens the Fairies skip and dance,
And Witches wallop o'er to France,
    Up in the Air
    On my bonny grey Mare.
And I see her yet, and I see her yet.

The Wind's drifting Hail and Sna'
O'er frozen Hags like a Foot Ba',
Nae Starns keek throw the Azure Slit,
'Tis cauld and mirk as ony Pit,
    The Man i' the Moon
    Is carowsing aboon,
D'ye see, d'ye see, d'ye see him yet.

Take your Glass to clear your Een,
'Tis the Elixir hales the Spleen,
Baith Wit and Mirth it will inspire,
And gently puffs the Lover's Fire,
    Up in the Air,
    It drives away Care,
Ha'e wi'ye, ha'e wi'ye, and ha'e wi'ye Lads yet.

Steek the Doors, keep out the Frost,
Come Willy gi'es about ye'r Tost,
Til't Lads, and lilt it out,
And let us ha'e a blythsom Bowt,
    Up wi't there, there,
    Dinna cheat, but drink fair,
Huzza, Huzza, and Huzza Lads yet.

Allan Ramsay (1684—1758)

# The Grey Selchie

An eart'ly nourris sits and sings,
And aye she sings, "Ba lily wean;
Little ken I my bairnis father,
Far less the land that he staps in."

Then ane arose at her bed fit,
An' a grimly guest I'm sure was he:
"Here am I thy bairnis father,
Although that I be not comelie.

"I am a man upo' the lan',
An' I am a silkie in the sea;
And when I'm far and far frae lan',
My dwelling is in Sule Skerrie."

"It was na weel," quo' the maiden fair,
"It was na weel, indeed," quo' she,
"That the Great Silkie of Sule Skerrie
S'uld ha'e come and aught a bairn to me."

Now he has ta'en a purse of gowd,
And he has pat it upo' her knee;
Sayin', "Gie to me my little young son,
An' tak' thee up thy nourris fee.

"An' it sall come to pass on a simmer's day
Quhen the sun shines het on evera stane,
That I will tak' my little young son,
An' teach him for to swim the faem.

"An' thu sall marry a proud gunner,
An' a proud gunner I'm sure he'll be;
An' the very first schot that e'er he schoots,
He'll schoot baith my young son and me."

# Thomas the Rhymer

True Thomas lay on Huntlie bank;
    A ferlie he spied wi' his e'e;
And there he saw a ladye bright
    Come riding down by the Eildon Tree.

Her skirt was o' the grass-green silk,
    Her mantle o' the velvet fyne;
At ilka tett o' her horse's mane
    Hung fifty siller bells and nine.

True Thomas he pu'd aff his cap,
    And louted low down on his knee:
"Hail to thee, Mary, Queen of Heaven!
    For thy peer on earth could never be."

"O no, O no, Thomas," she said,
    "That name does not belang to me;
I'm but the Queen o' fair Elfland,
    That am hither come to visit thee.

"Harp and carp, Thomas," she said;
    "Harp and carp along wi' me;
And if ye dare to kiss my lips,
    Sure of your bodie I will be."

"Betide me weal, betide me woe,
    That weird shall never daunten me."
Syne he has kiss'd her rosy lips,
    All underneath the Eildon Tree.

"Now ye maun go wi' me," she said,
    "True Thomas, ye maun go wi' me;
And ye maun serve me seven years,
    Thro' weal or woe as may chance to be."

She's mounted on her milk-white steed,
    She's ta'en true Thomas up behind;
And aye, whene'er her bridle rang,
    The steed gaed swifter than the wind.

O they rade on, and farther on,
    The steed gaed swifter than the wind;
Until they reach'd a desert wide,
    And living land was left behind.

"Light down, light down now, true Thomas,
    And lean your head upon my knee;
Abide ye there a little space,
    And I will show you ferlies three.

"O see ye not yon narrow road,
    So thick beset wi' thorns and briers?
That is the Path of Righteousness,
    Though after it but few inquires.

"And see ye not yon braid, braid road,
    That lies across the lily leven?
That is the Path of Wickedness,
    Though some call it the Road to Heaven.

"And see ye not yon bonny road
    That winds about the fernie brae?
That is the road to fair Elfland,
    Where thou and I this night maun gae.

"But, Thomas, ye sall haud your tongue,
    Whatever ye may hear or see;
For speak ye word in Elfyn-land,
    Ye'll ne'er win back to your ain countrie."

O they rade on, and farther on,
    And they waded rivers abune the knee;
And they saw neither sun nor moon,
    But they heard the roaring of the sea.

It was mirk, mirk night, there was nae starlight,
    They waded thro' red blude to the knee;
For a' the blude that's shed on the earth
    Rins through the springs o' that countrie.

Syne they came to a garden green,
    And she pu'd an apple frae a tree:
"Take this for thy wages, true Thomas;
    It will give thee the tongue that can never lee."

"My tongue is my ain," true Thomas he said;
    "A gudely gift ye wad gie to me!
I neither dought to buy or sell
    At fair or tryst where I might be.

"I dought neither speak to prince or peer,
    Nor ask of grace from fair ladye!" —
"Now haud thy peace, Thomas," she said,
    "For as I say, so must it be."

He has gotten a coat of the even cloth,
    And a pair o' shoon of the velvet green;
And till seven years were gane and past,
    True Thomas on earth was never seen.

## ■ Omens

I heard the cuckoo with no food in my stomach,
I heard the stock-dove on the top of the tree,
I heard the sweet singer in the copse beyond,
And I heard the screech of the owl of the night.

I saw the lamb with his back to me,
I saw the snail on the bare flag-stone,
I saw the foal with his rump to me,
I saw the wheatear on a dyke of holes,
I saw the snipe while sitting bent,
And I foresaw that the year would not
  Go well with me.

Translated from the Gaelic
by Alexander Carmichael

## ■ The Wife of Usher's Well

There lived a wife at Usher's Well
  And a wealthy wife was she;
She had three stout and stalwart sons
  And sent them o'er the sea.

They hadna been a week from her,
  A week but barely ane,
Whan word came to the carline wife
  That her three sons were gane.

They hadna been a week from her,
  A week but barely three,
Whan word came to the carline wife
  That her sons she'd never see.

I wish the wind may never cease,
   Nor fashes in the flood,
Till my three sons come hame to me
   In earthly flesh and blood.

It fell about the Martinmas
   Whan nights are lang and mirk,
The carline wife's three sons came hame
   And their hats were o' the birk.

It neither grew in syke nor ditch
   Nor yet in ony sheugh,
But at the gates o' Paradise
   That birk grew fair eneugh.

Blow up the fire, my maidens,
   Bring water from the well;
For a' my house shall feast this night
   Since my three sons are well.

And she has made to them a bed,
   She's made it large and wide,
And she's ta'en her mantle her about,
   Sat down at the bed-side.

Up then crew the red, red cock
   And up and crew the gray;
The eldest to the youngest said,
   'Tis time we were away.

The cock he hadna craw'd but once
   And clapp'd his wings at a'
Whan the youngest to the eldest said,
   Brother, we must awa'.

The cock doth craw, the day doth daw,
   The channerin' worm doth chide;
Gin we be mist out o' our place
   A sair pain we maun bide.

Fare ye weel, my mother dear;
Fareweel to barn and byre;
And fare ye weel, the bonny lass
That kindles my mother's fire.


# The Hazlewood Witch

For many lang year I ha'e heard frae my grannie
  Of brownies and bogles by yon castle wa',
Of auld withered hags that were never thought canny,
  And fairies that danced till they heard the cock craw.
I leugh at her tales, and last ouk, i' the gloaming
  I dandered, alane, down the Hazlewood green;
Alas! I was reckless, and rue sair my roaming,
  For I met a young witch wi' twa  bonnie black een.

I thought o' the starns in a frosty night glancing,
  Whan a' the lift round them is cloudless and blue;
I lookit again, and my heart fell a dancing;
  Whan I wad hae spoken she glamoured my mou',
O wae to her cantrips! for dumpish I wander;
  At kirk or at market there's nought to be seen;
For she dances afore me wherever I dander,
  The Hazlewood witch wi' the bonnie black een.

Richard Gall (1776—1801)

# Fine Flowers in the Valley

She sat down below a thorn,
    Fine flowers in the valley,
And there she has her sweet babe born
    And the green leaves they grow rarely.

Smile na sae sweet, my bonie babe
    Fine flowers in the valley,
And ye smile sae sweet, ye'll smile me dead,
    And the green leaves they grow rarely.

She's taen out her little penknife
    Fine flowers in the valley,
And twinn'd the sweet babe o' its life,
    And the green leaves they grow rarely.

She's howket a grave by the light o' the moon,
    Fine flowers in the valley,
And there she's buried her sweet babe in,
    And the green leaves they grow rarely.

As she was going to the church,
    Fine flowers in the valley,
She saw a sweet babe in the porch,
    And the green leaves they grow rarely.

O sweet babe and thou were mine,
    Fine flowers in the valley,
I wad cleed thee in the silk so fine
    And the green leaves they grow rarely.

O mother dear, when I was thine,
    Fine flowers in the valley,
You did na prove to me sae kind,
    And the green leaves they grow rarely.

Robert Burns (1759—1796)

## Index of First Lines and Ballad Titles

About ane bank, quhair birdis on bewis, 63
Ah! if yee aske (my friendes) why this salt shower, 85
Alas, poor Tom! how oft, with merry heart, 222
Alone on the hill-top, sadly and silently, 36
An eart'ly nourris sits and sings, 244
As I was walking all alane, 211
As Lady Marg'ret sat in her bow'r, 229
As Tam the Chapman on a day, 217
At that sweet period of revolving time, 102

BATTLE OF OTTERBOURNE, 146
Belive Eneas membris schuk for cald, 99
BESSIE BELL AND MARY GRAY, 218
Betuix twell houris and ellevin, 15
Blest be the boat, 108
Blythe, blythe and merry was she, 190
BONNIE GEORGE CAMPBELL, 161
BONNIE EARL O' MORAY, THE, 223
Brissit brawnis and broken banis, 129
By Logan's stream that rin sae deep, 37

'Come under my plaidie, the night's gaun to fa', 178
Cope sent a letter frae Dunbar, 156

Daft gowk, in macaroni dress, 69
Deep sunk in floods of grief, 201
Devoit peopill, gude day I say yow, 27
Did you ever see the day, 59
Did you hear from Cille-Cummin, 152
Done is a battell on the dragon blak, 197

EARL OF MAR'S DAUGHTER, THE, 238
Escaped the gloom of mortal life, a soul, 218
Esope myne authour makis mentioun, 74

Fair Candia now no more beneath her lee, 100
Fair fa' your honest sonsie face, 113
Fair maid, you need not take the hint, 21
First Iove, as greatest God aboue the rest, 56
For many lang year I ha'e heard frae my grannie, 250
Frae fields where Spring her sweets has blawn, 87

Go, fetch to me a pint o' wine, 159
Go shorn and come woolly, 82
Great, good, and just, could I but rate, 60
GREY SELCHIE, THE, 244

Hie upon Hielands and laigh upon Tay, 161
His Majesty, Heaven guide his Grace, 134
Ho! ho! ho! the foxes, 83

I come from heuin to tell, 193
I gaed a waefu' gate yestreen, 168
I heard the cuckoo with no food in my stomach, 248
I, Henry, hope with this mine eyes to feed, 58
I praise Thee, Christ, that on Thy breast, 202
I saw a stranger yestreen, 208
I saw the dun stag and the hinds, 132
I that in heill wes and gladness, 212
I'm wearin' awa', John, 216
In dulci jubilo, now let us sing with mirth and jo, 197
In Iona of my heart, Iona of my love, 38
It fell about the Lammas tide, 146
It was intil a pleasant time, 238
I've heard them lilting at our yowe-milking, 151

John Anderson my jo, John, 184

Lament him, Mauchline husbands a', 222
LAMENT OF THE BORDER WIDOW, THE, 224
Let a broad man, stout and brawny, 107
Let them bestow on every airth a limb, 215
LORD DONALD, 122
Love's like a Game at Tables, where your Dy, 173
LOWLANDS OF HOLLAND, THE, 106

Marie Hamilton's to the kirk gane, 53
Maxwelltown banks are bonnie, 172
My delight it was to rise, 30
My love he built me a bonny bower, 224
My love he's built a bonnie ship, and set her on the sea, 106
My lufe murnis for me, for me, 203
My Peggy is a young thing, 167

Now Israel may say, and that truly, 200
Now mirk December's dowie face, 33
Now, Priam's son, thou mayst be mute, 17
Now the Sun's gane out o' Sight, 243

O' a' the waters that can hobble, 117
O Alva hills is bonny, 38
O Bessie Bell and Mary Gray, 218
O Canningate! poor elritch Hole, 120
O cruell love, why dothe thow sore assayle, 169
O eterne God of power infinyt, 205
O happie death, to life the readie way, 216
O my Luve's like a red, red rose, 165
O Rair, 170
O that I were all soule that I might prove, 188
O Thou great Being! what Thou art, 204
O Thou, wha in the Heavens dost dwell, 24
O Waly, waly up the bank, 180
O, wert thou in the cauld blast, 171
Oh, my love's in Germany, send him hame, send him hame, 158
'Oh, where ha'e ye been all day, Lord Donald my son, 122
'Oh where, tell me where, is your Highland laddie gone, 160
On Scotia's plains, in days of yore, 135
Out of the south thai saw quhar at the queyn, 42

Pity one that bears love's anguish, 183
Poor turtle! thou bemoans, 175

QUEEN'S MARIE, THE, 53
Quhare in a lusty plane tuke I my way, 44
Quhen thay war seruit and set to the Suppar, 114

RARE WILLY DROWNED IN YARROW, 225
Rorate celi desuper, 195

Schir, sen that God, of his preordinance, 49
Schir, ye have mony servitouris, 46
Scots, wha hae wi' Wallace bled, 43
She sat down below a thorn, 251
Should I my steps turn to the rural seat, 68
SIR PATRICK SPENS, 95
SIR WILLIAM WALLACE, 21
So suete a kis yistrene fra thee I reft, 166
Sum wyfis of the burrows-toun, 17
SWEET WILLIAM'S GHOST, 229

Than Robene Roy begouth to revell, 130
That which I first for Henries life did sound, 60
The Catrine woods were yellow seen, 15

The golden globe incontinent, 65
The Inglis archeris schot sa fast, 145
The king sits in Dunfermline town, 95
The lipper folk to Cresseid than can draw, 176
The Lord's my shepherd, I'll not want, 199
The tender snow, of granis soft & quhȳt, 172
There lived a wife at Usher's Well, 248
There was ance a may, and she lo'ed na men, 174
There's fortune in't, we'll have a drink, 125
Think on god that the bocht, 202
This ae nighte, this ae nighte, 225
THOMAS THE RHYMER, 245
Tibby has a Store of Charms, 186
'Tis I, — dear Caledonians, blythsome Tony, 138
To luve unluvit it is ane pane, 185
True Thomas lay on Huntlie bank, 245
TWA CORBIES, THE, 211
Twa Travellers, as they were wa'king, 81

Vpon the vtmost corners of the warld, 35

Wee, modest, crimson tipped flow'r, 90
Wee, sleekit, cowrin, tim'rous Beastie, 72
Welcum, illustrat Ladye, and oure Quene, 52
Wha hes gud malt and makis ill drink, 124
Wha'll buy my caller herrin', 116
When Alysandyr our King was dede, 41
When Britain first, at heaven's command, 104
When chapman billies leave the street, 232
When Flora had ourfret the firth, 187
When the sheep are in the fauld, and the kye's a' at hame, 181
When trees did bud, and fields were green, 166
While sober folks, in humble prose, 219
Who knows your greatness, cannot but with fear, 57
Wi' a hundred pipers an' a', an' a', 155
WIFE OF USHER'S WELL, THE, 248
'Willy's rare, and Willy's fair, 225
With tramps, and brooms, and stones, a crowd now comes, 129
Wou'd ye hear of William Wallace, 21

Ye banks and braes o' bonnie Doon, 179
Ye few, whose feeling hearts are ne'er estranged, 139
Ye Highlands and ye Lawlands, 223
Ye hypocrites! are these your pranks, 161

# Index of Poets

Alexander, *Sir* William 58, 60

Ayton, *Sir* Robert 57, 59, 173, 188

Baillie, *Lady* Grisell 174
Barbour, John 145
Barnard, *Lady* Anne 182
Beattie, James 218
Blind Harry 42
Burns, Robert 15, 21, 24, 43, 72, 90, 113, 159, 161, 165, 168, 171, 179, 184, 190, 204, 217, 222, 232, 251

Crawford, Robert 166

Douglas, Gavin 99
Drummond, William, *of* Hawthornden 85, 175
Dunbar, William 15, 46, 195, 198, 212

Elliot, Jean 151

Falconer, William 100
Fergusson, Robert 33, 69, 87, 102, 117, 135, 141, 219, 222
Fingland, Douglas *of* 172
Fisher, James 129
Fowler, William 35, 169

Gall, Richard 250
Graham, James (Marquis of Montrose) 60, 215
Grant, Ann, *of* Laggan 160

Henryson, Robert 74, 176, 205

Hume, Alexander 67, 216

James I 44
James VI 56

Ker, Robert 201

Lom, Iain 152
Lyndsay, *Sir* David 27, 49

Macdonald, Alexander 107
MacIntyre, Duncan Ban 30, 83, 125, 133
Macleod, Mary 36
MacNeill, Hector 178
Maitland, *Sir* Richard 17
Mallet, David 104
Mayne, John 37
Montgomerie, Alexander 63, 166, 172
Muireadhach Albannach 202

Nairne, *Lady* 116, 155, 216

Ramsay, Allan 17, 81, 120, 134, 138, 167, 186, 243

Scott, Alexander 52, 185
Skirving, Adam 156
Stewart, Isabel 183
Stewart, John, *of* Baldynneis 170

Thomson, James 68
Traill, *Colonel* Thomas 158